# Bloom's BioCritiques

Dante Alighieri
Maya Angelou
Jane Austen
The Brontë Sisters
Lord Byron
Albert Camus
Geoffrey Chaucer
Anton Chekhov
Joseph Conrad
Stephen Crane
Charles Dickens
Emily Dickinson
T. S. Eliot
Ralph Ellison
William Faulkner
F. Scott Fitzgerald
Robert Frost
Nathaniel Hawthorne
Ernest Hemingway
Langston Hughes
Zora Neale Hurston
James Joyce
Stephen King
Arthur Miller
John Milton
Toni Morrison
Edgar Allan Poe
J. D. Salinger
William Shakespeare
John Steinbeck
Henry David Thoreau
Mark Twain
Alice Walker
Walt Whitman
Tennessee Williams
William Wordsworth

*Bloom's BioCritiques*

# NATHANIEL HAWTHORNE

*Edited and with an introduction by*
## Harold Bloom
Sterling Professor of the Humanities
Yale University

CHELSEA HOUSE
PUBLISHERS
A Haights Cross Communications Company

Philadelphia

©2003 by Chelsea House Publishers, a subsidiary of
Haights Cross Communications.

A Haights Cross Communications Company

Introduction © 2003 by Harold Bloom.

Printed and bound in the United States of America.

10  9  8  7  6  5  4  3  2  1

Library of Congress Cataloging-in-Publication Data

Nathaniel Hawthorne / edited and with an introduction by Harold Bloom.
        p. cm. -- (Bloom's biocritiques)
Includes bibliographical references and index.
  ISBN 0-7910-7383-1
 1.  Hawthorne, Nathaniel, 1904–1864--Criticism and interpretation.  I.
Bloom, Harold. II. Series.
  PS1888.N295 2003
  813'.3--dc21

                                                           2003001603

Chelsea House Publishers
1974 Sproul Road, Suite 400
Broomall, PA 19008-0914

http://www.chelseahouse.com

Contributing editor: Neil Heims

Cover design by Keith Trego

Cover: © Hulton Archive/Getty Images

Layout by EJB Publishing Services

# CONTENTS

# User's Guide

These volumes are designed to introduce the reader to the life and work of the world's literary masters. Each volume begins with Harold Bloom's essay "The Work in the Writer" and a volume-specific introduction also written by Professor Bloom. Following these unique introductions is an engaging biography that discusses the major life events and important literary accomplishments of the author under consideration.

Furthermore, each volume includes an original critique that not only traces the themes, symbols, and ideas apparent in the author's works, but strives to put those works into a cultural and historical perspective. In addition to the original critique is a brief selection of significant critical essays previously published on the author and his or her works followed by a concise and informative chronology of the writer's life. Finally, each volume concludes with a bibliography of the writer's works, a list of additional readings, and an index of important themes and ideas.

HAROLD BLOOM

# The Work in the Writer

Literary biography found its masterpiece in James Boswell's *Life of Samuel Johnson*. Boswell, when he treated Johnson's writings, implicitly commented upon Johnson as found in his work, even as in the great critic's life. Modern instances of literary biography, such as Richard Ellmann's lives of W. B. Yeats, James Joyce, and Oscar Wilde, essentially follow in Boswell's pattern.

That the writer somehow is in the work, we need not doubt, though with William Shakespeare, writer-of-writers, we almost always need to rely upon pure surmise. The exquisite rancidities of the Problem Plays or Dark Comedies seem to express an extraordinary estrangement of Shakespeare from himself. When we read or attend *Troilus and Cressida* and *Measure for Measure*, we may be startled by particular speeches of Ulysses in the first play, or of Vincentio in the second. These speeches, of Ulysses upon hierarchy or upon time, or of Duke Vincentio upon death, are too strong either for their contexts or for the characters of their speakers. The same phenomenon occurs with Parolles, the military impostor of *All's Well That Ends Well*. Utterly disgraced, he nevertheless affirms: "Simply the thing I am/Shall make me live."

In Shakespeare, more even than in his peers, Dante and Cervantes, meaning always starts itself again through excess or overflow. The strongest of Shakespeare's creatures—Falstaff, Hamlet, Iago, Lear, Cleopatra—have an exuberance that is fiercer than their plays can contain. If Ben Jonson was at all correct in his complaint that "Shakespeare wanted art," it could have been only in a sense that he may not have intended. Where do the personalities of Falstaff or Hamlet touch a limit? What was it in Shakespeare that made the two parts of *Henry IV* and *Hamlet* into "plays unlimited"? Neither Falstaff nor Hamlet will be stopped: their wit, their beautiful, laughing speech, their intensity of being—all these are virtually infinite.

In what ways do Falstaff and Hamlet manifest the writer in the work? Evidently, we can never know, or know enough to answer with any authority. But what would happen if we reversed the question, and asked: How did the work form the writer, Shakespeare?

Of Shakespeare's inwardness, his biography tells us nothing. And yet, to an astonishing extent, Shakespeare created our inwardness. At the least, we can speculate that Shakespeare so lived his life as to conceal the depths of his nature, particularly as he rather prematurely aged. We do not have Shakespeare on Shakespeare, as any good reader of the Sonnets comes to realize: they do not constitute a key that unlocks his heart. No sequence of sonnets could be less confessional or more powerfully detached from the poet's self.

The German poet and universal genius, Goethe, affords a superb contrast to Shakespeare. Of Goethe's life, we know more than everything; I wonder sometimes if we know as much about Napoleon or Freud or any other human being who ever has lived, as we know about Goethe. Everywhere, we can find Goethe in his work, so much so that Goethe seems to crowd the writing out, just as Byron and Oscar Wilde seem to usurp their own literary accomplishments. Goethe, cunning beyond measure, nevertheless invested a rival exuberance in his greatest works that could match his personal charisma. The sublime outrageousness of the Second Part of *Faust*, or of the greater lyric and meditative poems, form a Counter-Sublime to Goethe's own daemonic intensity.

Goethe was fascinated by the daemonic in himself; we can doubt that Shakespeare had any such interests. Evidently, Shakespeare abandoned his acting career just before he composed *Measure for Measure* and *Othello*. I surmise that the egregious interventions by Vincentio and Iago displace the actor's energies into a new kind of mischief-making, a fresh opening to a subtler playwriting-within-the-play.

But what had opened Shakespeare to this new awareness? The answer is the work in the writer, *Hamlet* in Shakespeare. One can go further: it was not so much the play, *Hamlet*, as the character Hamlet, who changed Shakespeare's art forever.

Hamlet's personality is so large and varied that it rivals Goethe's own. Ironically Goethe's Faust, his Hamlet, has no personality at all, and is as colorless as Shakespeare himself seems to have chosen to be. Yet nothing could be more colorful than the Second Part of *Faust*, which is peopled by an astonishing array of monsters, grotesque devils, and classical ghosts.

A contrast between Shakespeare and Goethe demonstrates that in each—but in very different ways—we can better find the work in the person, than we can discover that banal entity, the person in the work. Goethe to many of his contemporaries, seemed to be a mortal god. Shakespeare, so far as we know, seemed an affable, rather ordinary fellow, who aged early and became somewhat withdrawn. Yet Faust, though Mephistopheles battles for his soul, is hardly worth the trouble unless you take him as an idea and not as a person. Hamlet is nearly every-idea-in-one, but he is precisely a personality and a person.

Would Hamlet be so astonishingly persuasive if his father's ghost did not haunt him? Falstaff is more alive than Prince Hal, who says that the devil haunts him in the shape of an old fat man. Three years before composing the final *Hamlet*, Shakespeare invented Falstaff, who then never ceased to haunt his creator. Falstaff and Hamlet may be said to best represent the work in the writer, because their influence upon Shakespeare was prodigious. W.H. Auden accurately observed that Falstaff possesses infinite energy: never tired, never bored, and absolutely both witty and happy until Hal's rejection destroys him. Hamlet too has infinite energy, but in him it is more curse than blessing.

Falstaff and Hamlet can be said to occupy the roles in Shakespeare's invented world that Sancho Panza and Don Quixote possess in Cervantes's. Shakespeare's plays from 1610 on (starting with *Twelfth Night*) are thus analogous to the Second Part of Cervantes's epic novel. Sancho and the Don overtly jostle Cervantes for authorship in the Second Part, even as Cervantes battles against the impostor who has pirated a continuation of his work. As a dramatist, Shakespeare manifests the work in the writer more indirectly. Falstaff's prose genius is revived in the scapegoating of Malvolio by Maria and Sir Toby Belch, while Falstaff's darker insights are developed by Feste's melancholic wit. Hamlet's intellectual resourcefulness, already deadly, becomes poisonous in Iago and in Edmund. Yet we have not crossed into the deeper abysses of the work in the writer in later Shakespeare.

No fictive character, before or since, is Falstaff's equal in self-trust. Sir John, whose delight in himself is contagious, has total confidence both in his self-awareness and in the resources of his language. Hamlet, whose self is as strong, and whose language is as copious, nevertheless distrusts both the self and language. Later Shakespeare is, as it were, much under the influence both of Falstaff and of Hamlet, but they tug him in opposite directions. Shakespeare's own copiousness of language is well-nigh incredible: a vocabulary in excess of twenty-one thousand words, almost eighteen hundred of which he coined himself. And of his word-hoard, nearly half are used only once each, as though the perfect setting for each had been found, and need not be repeated. Love for language and faith in language are Falstaffian attributes. Hamlet will darken both that love and that faith in Shakespeare, and perhaps the Sonnets can best be read as Falstaff and Hamlet counterpointing against one another.

Can we surmise how aware Shakespeare was of Falstaff and Hamlet, once they had played themselves into existence? *Henry IV, Part I* appeared in six quarto editions during Shakespeare's lifetime; *Hamlet* possibly had four. Falstaff and Hamlet were played again and again at the Globe, but Shakespeare knew also that they were being read, and he must have had contact with some of those readers. What would it have been like to discuss Falstaff or Hamlet with one of their early readers (presumably also part of their audience at the Globe), if you were the creator of such demiurges? The question would seem nonsensical to most Shakespeare scholars, but then these days they tend to be either ideologues or moldy figs. How can we recover the uncanniness of Falstaff and of Hamlet, when they now have become so familiar?

A writer's influence upon himself is an unexplored problem in criticism, but such an influence is never free from anxieties. The biocritical problem (which this series attempts to explore) can be divided into two areas, difficult to disengage fully. Accomplished works affect the author's life, and also affect her subsequent writings. It is simpler for me to surmise the effect of *Mrs. Dalloway* and *To the Lighthouse* upon Woolf's late *Between the Acts*, than it is to relate Clarissa Dalloway's suicide and Lily Briscoe's capable endurance in art to the tragic death and complex life of Virginia Woolf.

There are writers whose lives were so vivid that they seem sometimes to obscure the literary achievement: Byron, Wilde, Malraux, Hemingway. But most major Western writers do not live that exuberantly, and the greatest of all, Shakespeare, sometimes appears to have adopted the personal mask of colorlessness. And yet there are heroes of literature who struggled titanically with their own eras—Tolstoy, Milton, Victor Hugo—who nevertheless matter more for their works than their lives.

There are great figures—Emily Dickinson, Wallace Stevens, Willa Cather—who seem to have had so little of the full intensity of life when compared to the vitality of their work, that we might almost speak of the work in the work, rather than even of the work in a person. Emily Brontë might well be the extreme instance of such a visionary, surpassing William Blake in that one regard.

I conclude this general introduction to a series of literary bio-critiques by stating a tentative formula or principle for gauging the many ways in which the work influences the person and her subsequent, later work. Our influence upon ourselves is always related to the Shakespearean invention of self-overhearing, which I have written about in several other contexts. Life, as well as poetry and prose, is overheard rather than simply heard. The writer listens to herself as though she were somebody else, and the will to change begins to operate. The forces that live in us include the prior work we have done, and the dreams and waking visions that evade our dismissals.

HAROLD BLOOM

# *Introduction*

Hawthorne's great novels—*The Scarlet Letter* and *The Marble Faun*—and the most extraordinary of his stories, including "Wakefield" and "Feathertop"—seem visions of an inner reality otherwise unrevealed to him. They are less allegories of his life than they are demonstrations of how his works formed his life, and imbued his spirit with qualities still unique in imaginative literature.

I will take the story, "Wakefield," regarded by Jorge Luis Borges as his favorite, as my exemplary instance of Hawthorne's imagination forming his life. Just seven pages or so, "Wakefield" is a story without a story. Wakefield, a Londoner, dwells for twenty years in a house a street away from his own, with no explanation to his wife. Until—"he entered the door one evening, quietly, as from a day's absence, and became a loving spouse till death."

That is all. The rest is Hawthorne's uncanny meditation upon Wakefield, which I find about as upsetting as a purely literary reflection can be:

> Amid the seeming confusion of our mysterious world, individuals are so nicely adjusted to a system, and systems to one another, and to a whole, that, by stepping aside for a moment, a man exposes himself to a fearful risk of losing his place forever. Like Wakefield, he may become, as it were, the Outcast of the Universe.

But Wakefield must, belatedly, come home to his wife. Though she, poor woman, took him in, Hawthorne is unforgiving. Even after his return, Wakefield remains the Outcast of the Universe, in a sense that Chillingworth, in *The Scarlet Letter*, was not. Chillingworth's sadistic relationship to Dimmesdale remained a relationship, morally horrible. Wakefield, who left for no reason and returns without cause, has fallen out of the world of relationship. For Hawthorne, there is no greater horror. His friend, Herman Melville, who adored Hawthorne, would not have agreed, though Ahab is no Wakefield.

NORMA JEAN LUTZ

# Biography of Nathaniel Hawthorne

## NEW ENGLAND ROOTS

The Hawthornes of New England traced their lineage to John Winthrop's historic Massachusetts Bay Colony, having arrived in the 1630s and settled in Dorchester. (Author, Nathaniel Hawthorne was the one who restored the original "w" to the name.) Eventually, the Hawthornes migrated to the great sailing port of Salem and became a seafaring family. A notable exception in the group was Judge John Hawthorne, who presided as one of the judges in the infamous Salem witch trials. Legend has it that one of the victims, just before her execution, placed a curse on the judge and his descendants. The curse is referred to by Nathaniel Hawthorne in his preface to *The Scarlet Letter.*

The grandson of Judge Hawthorne, Daniel, born in 1731, achieved fame as a privateer during the Revolutionary War. In command of his ship, *True American*, Daniel was wounded in a battle, in which three crew members were killed and ten others wounded. A ballad of the times, entitled "Bold Daniel," is based on his exploits. Daniel and his wife, Rachael had seven children, one of whom, Nathaniel, was the father and namesake of the famous author. Three of Daniel's daughters married wealthy sea merchants, ushering them into the upper society of Salem's elite. Daniel, named for his father, was also a master and owner of ships. Nathaniel, also a sailor, apparently did not experience the same success as his family members.

By age twenty, Nathaniel had gone to sea but never became a ship owner, but instead sailed ships of other wealthy men. Perhaps his heart was not in the seafaring life. He was said to be "a great reader, employing all his leisure time at sea over books" [Mellow 12]. Journals that he kept, and that later came into his son's hands, showed a man marking time and writing poetic couplets. On August 2, 1801, Nathaniel married Elizabeth Clarke Manning, whom he called Betsey.

The Manning family was equally as successful as the Hawthornes, but in a different manner. Elizabeth Manning Hawthorne came from a family of nine children; she was the first of the children to get married. Her father, Richard Manning, Jr., was an established blacksmith in Salem. Being a shrewd businessman, he added a livery stable, which eventually grew into a highly profitable stagecoach line between Boston and Salem. The stage line was later run by Betsey's brothers. Richard also purchased large tracts of land in Cumberland County, Maine on the shores of Lake Sebago. He spent a good deal of time in the area, which his family referred to as "the land of promise." When Richard Manning died in 1813, the job of managing the family fortune fell to his sons, Robert and Richard III.

Following the marriage of Nathaniel Hawthorne, Sr., and Elizabeth Manning, the couple made their home in a gray, hip-roofed house on Union Street owned by Nathaniel's father. The household was made up of Nathaniel's mother, his two unmarried sisters, and brother Daniel who was out to sea as often as Nathaniel. Their first child, a daughter Elizabeth, arrived seven months after the marriage, the shame of which some would say, caused Elizabeth to seclude herself later in life. While the Captain was on another voyage, his namesake, Nathaniel, made his appearance on Independence Day, July 4, 1804. Four years later, when a second daughter, Maria Louisa was born, Captain Hawthorne was sailing for the West Indies. While his ship, the *Nabby*, was docked at Surinam (Dutch Guiana) and awaiting clearance for departure, yellow fever struck the crew. Captain Hawthorne died and was buried there.

When the *Nabby* returned to Salem, Captain Hawthorne's clothing and other belongings were given to his widow, Elizabeth. Among them she found the list of his final expenses, which included fees for the physician, the coffin, the minister, and the digging of the grave. Although he had sailed in January, the family did not receive word of his death until April 1808. Daughter Elizabeth, called "Ebe" because of her little brother's inability to pronounce her name, remembered being told of their father's death:

I remember very well that one morning, my mother called my brother into her room, next to the one where we slept, and told him that his father was dead. He left very little property and my Grandfather Manning took us home. [Mellow 14]

For whatever reason, Elizabeth chose to leave the home of the Hawthornes and return to the home of the Mannings, a move within the same neighborhood, but one that would forever change and mold the life of young Nathaniel Hawthorne.

The Manning house on Herbert Street fairly burst at the seams with busy, outgoing people. The business of running a successful stage line required the attention of Grandfather Manning and his two older sons, Robert and Richard. Two younger uncles, only a few years older than Ebe, were wonderful playmates. The older aunts and uncles became surrogate parents to Ebe, Hawthorne, and Louisa, as did the grandparents. Ebe, in her latter years, recalled the affection they received:

We were indulged in all convenient ways, and under very little control, except that of circumstances. There were aunts and uncles, and they were all as fond, especially of your father, and as careful of his welfare, as if he had been their own child. [Mellow 15]

The Manning home offered a large garden area graced with tall trees and flowering shrubs, which served as a perfect playground. Hawthorne played there tirelessly with younger sister, Louisa, rolling her about in a little cart. While he admired his older sister, Ebe tended to be domineering; Hawthorne formed a closer friendship with his younger sister, Louisa.

In her deep grief over the loss of her husband, Hawthorne's mother cloistered herself in a cold, darkened north room upstairs and seldom came out. In that room, she took her meals and busied herself with reading, sewing and overseeing the care of her children. She received guests and family members graciously, but apparently felt no need from that time forward to enter into the outside world. She also felt no inclination to maintain contact with her husband's family;

therefore, Hawthorne grew up having few close relationships to his father's side of the family. He remembered going to Grandmother Hawthorne's on Sunday afternoons to read, usually from *Pilgrim's Progress*, which was considered acceptable reading material for Sunday. His knowledge of the Hawthorne heritage came only after a study of New England history when he was a grown man.

Uncle Robert, third in line of the four Manning sons, became the self-appointed guardian for Hawthorne, a role in which he delighted. A bachelor for many years, Robert did not marry until he was forty. Throughout his life he took increasing interest in the cultivation of fruit trees and developed extensive orchards in Salem and in Maine. By his death in 1842, he was regarded as America's leading pomologist. While tending to the family property in Maine he wrote a letter to his nephew that openly expressed his affection:

> Nathaniel—O how I am bedear'd and beuncle'd by great Boys and girls. Why, when I read your letter, I went to the glass to see my white hairs, I felt as if I was 40 or 50 years old, but no matter for that, be good children and the older 'Dear Uncle' grows, the more he will love you. Nat, you want to learn to swim, and so you shall when Uncle comes home, but you must study the hard lessons, learn all you can at school, mind your mother, don't look cross, hold up your head like a man, keep your cloth[e]s clean, and when Uncle comes home we shall enjoy ourselves as we did in good old times. [Mellow 16]

Future letters would show that while Hawthorne chafed some under his uncle's leadership, he gave his Uncle Robert the respect due him and never openly rebelled.

Of Hawthorne's relationship to his Grandfather Manning, we know very little, only that he regarded his grandfather as a "kindly figure." The spring before Hawthorne turned nine, his grandfather left Salem to go to Raymond, Maine, to manage his properties there. On the way, he died in his sleep of an apoplectic stroke while staying overnight at Newburyport. Thus, another father figure was cruelly taken from young Hawthorne's life.

CAREFREE YEARS

Following the death of Hawthorne's grandfather, his Uncle Richard moved to Maine to manage the family real estate there. Suffering from a crippling disease, Richard was forced to use crutches for most of his life and before he died was confined to a wheel chair. The disease left him a bitter man. In a letter to Hawthorne's mother, he said, "As to my lameness, I have given over all thoughts of ever getting better of that, but I do not forget to complain of my hard fortune, and very often, curse the day in which I was born" [Mellow 16]. In spite of the lameness, he managed a store which he opened in Raymond, and eventually married at the age of thirty-three. His decision to live permanently in Raymond eventually affected the other members of the family, who occasionally considered moving the entire household away from Salem to the wilderness of Maine.

By the age of six, Hawthorne was sent to school, and while he loved to read—learning how to at a very young age—he had no affection for school. As an adult he referred to it as "a grievous disinclination to go to school" [Hawthorne 95]. He was attending the school of Joseph Emerson Worcester when in November 1813, he broke his foot playing ball with the other boys. The accident proved to be much more serious than was initially thought. After a month out of school, Hawthorne was still unable to walk. A local doctor attended him, and later a second doctor was consulted but with no promising results. The family was quite concerned. In a letter to her Uncle Robert, Ebe appealed to him about the matter: "I don't know as Nathaniel's foot will ever get well if you don't come home, he won't walk on it, and the doctor says he must; so do come home soon" [Mellow 19].

During his confinement, Hawthorne contented himself by reading many books of his own choosing. After a month or so, Mr. Worcester, his instructor came to hear his lessons, but perhaps not often enough to suit Hawthorne's Aunt Priscilla. In a letter to Robert, she seemed disturbed, pleading with him to insist that Hawthorne keep up his studies. "Be so good Robert as to favour him with your advice (which I think will not fail to be influential) with regard to attending to writing, and some of his lessons, regularly" [Mellow 19]. Ebe would later state that it was during this time that her brother acquired his love for books and for solitude. While Hawthorne may have enjoyed the attention and the freedom away from school, by the following summer, he was greatly disappointed to have missed the Independence Day celebration in which he always took great delight. Toward the end of the summer, Aunt Priscilla reported that his foot appeared to be improving. Not until January 1815, however, could Hawthorne's mother write an even better report to her brother Richard. "Nathaniel has entirely recovered the use of his foot," she wrote, "and walks as well as he did before he was lame. His joy was great when he found he could walk without his crutches. It is indeed a subject of thankfulness to us all" [Mellow 20].

Increasingly more Manning family activities took place at Raymond. For a time Hawthorne's mother and her spinster sister, Mary, considered purchasing a farm near Raymond, but the plans never fully developed. The Hawthornes did stay as boarders with a farm family for a short time during the summer of 1816—long enough for them to know they liked the area very much. Robert built a house near Lake Sebago outside Raymond, the size of which would accommodate any family members who wanted to live there. After the house was completed, Betsey and her children moved to Maine in 1818 and lived in Robert's house for almost a year. Hawthorne would look back upon the time as some of the happiest moments of his life:

> [H]ere I ran quite wild, and would, I doubt not, have willingly run wild till this time, fishing all day long, or shooting with an old fowling-piece; but reading a good deal, too, on the rainy days, especially in Shakespeare and 'The Pilgrim's Progress,' and any poetry or light books within my reach. Those were delightful days; for that part of the country was wild then, with only scattered clearings, and nine tenths of it primeval woods. [Hawthorne J. 96]

The area offered hunting and fishing as well as places in which to swim in summer and ice skate in winter. There were flowers and plants Hawthorne had never seen before and animals and birds to watch. It never mattered to him whether he went with friends or alone because he was always quite content to be by himself. Years later, in a letter to his publisher, he remarked that he had lived in Maine "like a bird of the air" [Turner 21].

Although the area was thinly settled, Hawthorne had a few friends, namely Robinson Cook, Jacob Dingley, and William Symmes. Jacob

Dingley, the younger brother of Uncle Richard's wife, went with Hawthorne that winter to a boarding school held at Stroudwater, a suburb of Portland. The school, taught by Reverend Caleb Bradley, was so unpopular with the two boys that in February they left the school and came home of their own accord. Accounts vary as to whether Hawthorne was sent back to complete the term. Suffice it to say, his uncle began to seriously consider sending him back to Salem to ensure that his education would be complete. Hawthorne was very disappointed. In a letter to his Uncle Robert dated May 16, 1819, he commented: "I am sorry you intend to send me to school again" [Turner 22]. Later that summer, he tried another ploy writing that "Mother says she can hardly spare me" [Turner 24]. Hawthorne's protests fell on deaf ears. At the age of thirteen, he had already received more education than any of his relatives. That Robert Manning insisted on further education for his nephew demonstrated his confidence in the boy's abilities. Perhaps he sensed the potential within Hawthorne.

Reluctantly returning to Salem, Hawthorne came under the watchful care of Aunt Mary, who could be a stern taskmaster, and his Grandmother Manning. Aunt Mary sewed his school clothes and saw that his lessons were completed. Uncle Robert arrived back in Salem and resumed charge of Hawthorne. By July 6, he was enrolled in Mr. Archer's school on Marlborough Street and was quite unhappy, missing his family and the freedom he had been forced to give up. Trying to put on a brave front, he wrote to his mother, "I am as well contented here as I expected to be, but sometimes I do have very bad fits of homesickness" [Mellow 22]. By September, he wrote to Louisa that he would "never be contented" in Salem.

Unlike his aunts, uncles and grandmother, Hawthorne's mother always guided her children with a gentle hand. Living in the Manning household with his mother many miles away, his life underwent changes, which deeply disturbed him. In March, he wrote his mother:

> I am extremely homesick. Aunt Mary is continually scolding at me. Grandma'am hardly ever speaks a pleasant word to me. If I ever attempt to speak a word in my defense, they cry out against my impudence. However, I guess I can live through a year and a half more, and then I shall leave them. One good effect results from their eternal finding-fault. It

gives me some employment in retaliating, and that keeps up
my spirits. [Mellow 23]

The last sentence indicates that he maintained a sense of humor. In
another letter Hawthorne lamented over the fact that his grandmother
had a pot of preserved limes in the pantry, which she kept in case
someone fell ill. Hawthorne remarked how disappointed Grandmother
would be if everyone remained well and the limes should spoil. "We have
some oranges too," he added, "which are rotting as fast as possible and
we stand a very fair chance of not having any good of them because we
have to eat the bad ones first, as the good are to be kept till they are
spoilt also" [Turner 31].

Amidst this gloom, there was a bright spot—Louisa was sent back
to Salem. Hawthorne suggested to his mother that Louisa go to live with
Aunt Priscilla, who was now married to John Dike, so she wouldn't have
to suffer under Aunt Mary's domineering hand. His suggestion was
ignored. Louisa's return in the summer of 1820 gave Hawthorne a
needed distraction. The two played shuttlecocks and battledores with
one another and were allowed to attend dance school together.
Hawthorne's comments about dancing indicate he enjoyed the pastime
and was willing to escort Louisa to a formal ball. While Aunt Mary felt
dancing to be a waste of time and money, Uncle William came forth with
the funds to sponsor the activity.

Hawthorne and Louisa, in a great display of fun and cooperation,
formed what they called the Pin Society. The organization had by-laws,
dues (one pin), two members, and an official publication, which they
named the *Spectator*. Through the *Spectator*, of which "N. Hawthorne"
was editor, many facets of Hawthorne's emerging personality were
revealed, including wit, irony, and fun-loving subtle humor. The paper,
neatly hand-printed by Hawthorne, offered writings by both siblings
and included news, advertisements and editorials. In referring to himself
as a literary man, he noted in one of his essays that "wealth does not lie
in the path of literature" [Turner 28]. His later life would bear out this
truth.

The paper's intended audience was the family members in
Raymond, allowing the younger Hawthornes to poke fun at their elders.
One classified ad read: "WANTED, A HUSBAND, not above seventy
years of age. None need apply unless they can produce GOOD

RECOMMENDATIONS or are possessed of at least TEN thousand DOLLARS. The Applicant is YOUNG, being under FIFTY years of age, and of GREAT BEAUTY. Mary Manning, Spinstress" [Turner 29]. One has to wonder how his spinster aunt took the joke.

Soon, his time at Mr. Arthur's school was finished, and Hawthorne began preparation for college under the tutelage of Benjamin Lynde Oliver, a Salem attorney. In the mornings, he studied at home and in the afternoons he worked as a bookkeeper for his Uncle William in the stage office. Evenings found him at the Lynde mansion at Essex and Liberty streets where Attorney Oliver lived. Hawthorne would give his recitations at Oliver's home. While Oliver believed Hawthorne would be ready for college by the fall, Uncle Robert thought he should wait one more year. He did not want his nephew to enter college under a handicap.

As the time to leave for college grew near, and after Ebe had returned to Salem, Hawthorne felt a bit of a panic that his mother might leave Raymond also, which meant his wilderness refuge would be lost forever. "I hope Dear Mother," he wrote in June of 1821, "that you will not be tempted by any entreaties to come to Salem to live. You can never have so much comfort here as you now enjoy. You are now undisputed Mistress of your own House.... If you remain where you are, think how delightfully the time will pass, with your children around you, shut out from the world, and nothing to disturb us. It will be a second Garden of Eden" [Hawthorne, H. 52]. Hawthorne's comments reveal that he was not thinking of his mother at all—a woman now living all alone—but of his own desires to once again enjoy the wilderness area around Raymond.

Life at Raymond was not the only worry Hawthorne struggled with before departing for college. His future vocation was being discussed by the entire family, and he was still uncertain of the path he would follow. Hawthorne made it clear in a letter to his mother that being a minister was out of the question. As to being a lawyer, he said there were already too many of them, and since he did not want to be exposed to infirmity and disease, the role of doctor was also excluded. Then he added these poignant words: "Oh that I was rich enough to live without a profession! What do you think of my becoming an author, and relying for support upon my pen? ... How proud you would feel to see my works praised by the reviewers" [Hawthorne, J. 108]. The daring proclamation revealed that the idea was already more than just a passing thought in his mind.

The family's choice of college for Hawthorne was Bowdoin, located in Brunswick, Maine, only a short distance from Raymond. While the curriculum was similar to that of Harvard, the tuition was much less. Bowdoin had opened its doors in 1802, two years prior to Hawthorne's birth, with only eight students. Upon his arrival in 1821, enrollment had swelled to 114. The village of Brunswick lay thirty miles from Portland and offered the same type of rural flavor that Hawthorne had known and enjoyed at Raymond. Whether or not Hawthorne felt he was ready for college, he and Uncle Robert boarded a stagecoach at Salem on September 28, 1821, bound for Brunswick, Maine.

## THE CHAMBER UNDER THE EAVES

As the stage lumbered toward Maine, it stopped along the way to pick up three more young men destined for Bowdoin. Alfred Mason and Jonathan Cilley were from Maine and entering their freshman year together. Franklin Pierce of New Hampshire was returning for his sophomore year. By the time they arrived, the four had become well acquainted with each other, although Hawthorne remained the quietest and most reserved of the four.

Upon arrival at the school, Hawthorne insisted that Uncle Robert stay until after the admission test had been administered. He was so concerned about passing that he wanted to be sure someone was on hand to take him directly back home if necessary. His concerns were put to rest when he passed the test and was assigned a room and a roommate. Before nightfall, Hawthorne became a full-fledged college student.

Franklin Pierce, a few months younger than Hawthorne in age, was a friendly outgoing young man, who exhibited leadership qualities. The son of the Revolutionary hero, General Benjamin Pierce, Franklin studied for law and later moved easily into the world of politics. Pierce's quiet confidence seemed to draw out the diffident Hawthorne, and the two became lifelong friends. Alfred Mason became Hawthorne's roommate and the two formed a warm continuing friendship. Mason, in turn, introduced Hawthorne to another law student, Horatio Bridge. With Bridge, Hawthorne came into a type of friendship that only strengthened with the passing of years. Horatio Bridge, more than any other person, aside from Hawthorne's future wife, seemed to sense the greatness that lay hidden within Hawthorne. A lawyer and politician, Bridge's father served as probate judge in Maine, no doubt encouraging Bridge to follow in his footsteps. The younger Bridge went on to enjoy a distinguished career in government.

Bowdoin produced its share of distinguished students, one of whom was Calvin Stowe. This star scholar of Pierce's class went on to become a noted preacher. He was best known after his wife, Harriet Beecher Stowe, wrote and published *Uncle Tom's Cabin* in 1850. Henry Wadsworth Longfellow, a member of Hawthorne's class, did not arrive until his sophomore year. He would later become the most beloved poet of his day. Upon Longfellow's graduation from Bowdoin, he was offered a position as professor of modern languages. While Hawthorne and Longfellow were not close in school, they developed a friendship in later years.

Hawthorne's studies at Bowdoin focused on Greek, Latin and mathematics, with some instruction on modern languages, literature, and history. Since most of the faculty had trained for the ministry, students were required to attend chapel twice a day. While Hawthorne disliked chapel, he disliked weekly declamations even more. Because of his aversion to public speaking, he opted to pay fines rather than give his presentations. Later in life, when he served as consul at Liverpool, Hawthorne made after-dinner speeches and surprised himself at how well he did. Still, he never enjoyed the experience and vowed after leaving office that he would never again raise his voice "so as to be heard by more than six people, nor to speak more than a hundred words together" [Turner 39]. In spite of his reluctance to speak in public, he joined an informal club made up of students who met as a tavern at the edge of the campus. There he willingly took part in oral recitations of essays and poetry.

Not the most rebellious student on campus, Hawthorne nevertheless joined in card games and other activities, which were against the rules, and faced suspension if he were caught. Fines assigned to Nathaniel Hawthorne's account in his first two years were for boyish pranks. In his third year they were mainly for failure to turn in class compositions. His senior year passed with few fines received at all. Perhaps by that time, Hawthorne had begun to sense the seriousness of his schoolwork or felt a sense of responsibility toward Uncle Robert, his benefactor.

When Hawthorne first arrived at school, his letters to his mother spoke often of the possibility of coming home for a visit; later the subject hardly ever came up. His first vacation spent at Raymond from mid-December to early February may have proved disappointing to him. Two and a half years had passed since the idyllic days spent there in his youth. In 1822, his mother moved back to Salem permanently. When Hawthorne visited Raymond one last time in the spring of 1825 prior to his graduation in the fall, he wrote to Ebe that he had no desire to return.

Fellow students at Bowdoin remembered Hawthorne as a shy, quiet person. Even when he was present among them, he held a measure of reservation, which kept him from opening up fully to any of his friends. One of his closest friends, Jonathan Cilley, remarked, "I love Hawthorne; I admire him; but I do not know him. He lives in a mysterious world of thought and imagination which he never permits me to enter" [Turner 40]. In spite of his quiet manners, Hawthorne was a person whom other students admired and wanted to be near, and he was included in all their activities.

Hawthorne's own assessment of his college years was not quite as glowing. "I was an idle student," he said, "negligent of college rules and the Procrustean details of academic life, rather choosing to nurse my own fancies than to dig into Greek roots and be numbered among the learned Thebans" [Mellow 31]. When graduation day arrived on September 7, 1825, Hawthorne was informed that he would graduate, but due to his failure to take part in declamation, he would not be allowed to speak at the ceremony. Since he had no desire to speak, the situation pleased him. He was just thankful to have made it to graduation—eighteenth in a class of thirty-eight. As far as can be ascertained, no family members attended his graduation.

That no one demanded Hawthorne immediately take up a salaried vocation says much for all of his Manning relatives. Comments made in various family letters reveal they all had a sense he was a gifted young man. In the year of Hawthorne's graduation, Uncle Robert married Rebecca Burnham, a second cousin in the Manning family, and Grandmother Miriam Manning passed away. After that, steps were taken to divide the Manning inheritance, which was sizeable. Due to the wealth of the Manning land holdings, Hawthorne's mother had lived rent-free throughout her years of widowhood. Now, because of what he would later refer to as "some slender means of supporting myself," Hawthorne was free to remain at home in the house on Herbert Street and "consider what pursuit in life I was best fit for" [Mellow 37]. This time of "considering," as he put it, would cover a span of twelve years. Of course, much more than "considering" took place in the "chamber under the eaves" as Hawthorne studied, read, and tried his hand at writing.

Looking back on this time of discipline and seclusion, Hawthorne was of two opinions about it. On the one hand, he saw it as a time when he was cheerful and healthy, and the seclusion did not adversely affect him. In a moment of opposing thoughts he said he had "sat a long, long time, waiting patiently for the world to know me, and sometimes wondering why it did not know me sooner, or whether it would ever know me at all—at least, till I were in my grave. And sometimes ... it seemed as if I were already in my grave" [Mellow 37]. Hawthorne's life fell into a pattern of writing in the daytime and taking long walks in the evening. He also read voraciously. Using his Aunt Mary's library card, Hawthorne would ask Ebe to fetch books for him. He dug deep into New England history and learned for the first time of the great heritage of the Hawthorne family. He was also especially fond of reading biographies and autobiographies.

Hawthorne's mother and sister, Elizabeth were also of a reclusive nature, and sometimes he and Ebe would not see one another for months at a time. "We do not live at our house," he once said, "we only vegetate. Elizabeth never leaves her den; I have mine in the upper story" [Mellow 39]. When they did spend time with one another, they often disagreed, especially in the area of politics. Ebe was highly opinionated. Louisa was the more outgoing of the whole family, and Hawthorne's relationship with her was more congenial. The two sometimes invited friends in for evenings to play cards.

Hawthorne was never able to write much during the summer, since he spent those months traveling. He gathered thoughts and observations in his journals, using them as source material for later writings. Several trips were taken with his Uncle Samuel. The two seemed to get along well, despite the fact that Samuel enjoyed spending time in taverns. When the first frost arrived and the leaves began to turn color, Hawthorne was back in his chamber again prepared to write. Steadily he moved forward, honing his skills with no one to guide him.

Frustration and discouragement were constant companions. Hawthorne burned much of the work he produced during that time. The subject of burning his writings later appeared in both his manuscripts and letters. To his close friend Horatio Bridge, he confessed his sense of failure as an author. He wrote to Bridge that he had destroyed his manuscripts "in a mood half savage, half despairing" [Mellow 45].

Putting together a group of stories in a collection, which he called *Seven Tales of My Native Land*, Hawthorne sent them to Ferdinand Andrews, a joint-owner of the *Salem Gazette*. Andrews agreed that the tales should be published; however, after a long delay, Hawthorne grew frustrated and asked them to be returned. Andrews later admitted he was waiting for his business to improve before taking on the project and did not want to let them go. In his disappointment and frustration, Hawthorne destroyed much of the work. In October, 1828, four years after his college graduation, Hawthorne published his novel, *Fanshawe*, at his own expense. The work was bought out by the Boston publisher Marsh and Capen for the price of $100, but with no name on the work. After the book's publication, several good reviews appeared in magazines and newspapers. One exception was a harsh review featured in the *Galaxy*, which Hawthorne agreed was his own view of the book. Several years after it had been issued, he asked for copies back from friends and family members and then destroyed them. For the rest of his life, he insisted that no one reveal his identity as the author of the book. *Fanshawe* did, however, put him in touch with Samuel G. Goodrich, a Boston publisher, who took an interest in Hawthorne's work. Goodrich used several of Hawthorne's sketches for his annual magazine, *The Token*, published every autumn. At Hawthorne's request, the sketches were published anonymously. In spite of the fact that Goodrich felt the writing was excellent, payment was meager.

While Hawthorne was working on his writing, his friend, Franklin Pierce was elected as speaker in the New Hampshire legislature. Writing to congratulate Pierce, Hawthorne wrote almost prophetically that the young politician would advance up the ranks to national politics. His prophecy stopped just short of suggesting that Pierce might become President.

In 1836, Goodrich recommended Hawthorne as an editor for the Boston-based *American Magazine of Useful and Entertaining Knowledge*. Hawthorne moved to Boston upon accepting his first employment since working in his uncle's stage office. Had circumstances been different, he might have held the post for a longer period, balancing his own writing with the work. However, the company was in dire straits and finally went bankrupt. After several months of extremely hard work and going without pay, Hawthorne resigned the position and returned to Salem. Horatio Bridge had expressed great joy when he first learned that Hawthorne was leaving Salem to work in Boston. "There is a peculiar dullness about Salem," Bridge wrote, "a heavy atmosphere which no literary man can breathe" [Mellow 74]. Upon hearing of Hawthorne's return to Salem, Bridge became concerned and wrote a number of encouraging letters one of which stated that "Brighter days will come, and that within six months" [Mellow 74].

Bridge was actively involved in making Hawthorne's words become a reality on the printed page. Hawthorne had decided to work with Goodrich on a collection of his stories entitled, *Twice-Told Tales*. Without Hawthorne's knowledge, Bridge corresponded with Goodrich, promising to post a guaranty of $250 for the work. The contract was issued and the deal was finalized. In a letter, Bridge broached the subject of Hawthorne's practice of not putting his name on his work: "I hope to God that you will put your name upon the title page, and come before the world at once and on your own responsibility. You could not fail to make a noise and an honorable name, and something besides" [Mellow 74]. In yet another letter, Bridge boldly stated, "The bane of your life had been self-distrust" [Mellow 76].

At last, Hawthorne took his friend's advice. *Twice-Told Tales* was published on March 6, 1837 and would bring Hawthorne's name to the reading public, and in an indirect way, also bring a special woman into his life.

## The Peabodys

The family of Dr. Nathaniel Peabody lived on Charter Street in a house overlooking the Salem cemetery—a setting later used in one of Hawthorne's books. Dr. Peabody was a dentist and his wife, Elizabeth, a teacher. They had six children: three daughters followed by three sons. Two sons died within a year of one another in 1838 and 1839. The third, Nathaniel Jr., was a pharmacist in Boston. Of the daughters, Elizabeth was the eldest, Mary Tyler was next, and Sophia was the youngest.

Elizabeth, highly educated, intellectual, inquisitive, and somewhat of a busybody, had read some of the anonymous stories of Nathaniel Hawthorne in the 1830s. Learning that the author was one of the very Hawthornes who were neighbors to the Peabodys—she first assumed the stories came from the pen of Ebe, Hawthorne's older sister. Lizzie Peabody remembered Ebe from their childhood days when she considered Ebe to be somewhat of a genius. Realizing a talented author lived in such close proximity, Lizzie decided to make a social call on the Hawthornes. Once there, she learned from Louisa that the author was not Ebe after all, but her brother. This new fact piqued Lizzie's fancy more than ever. When informed that Hawthorne had been living the life of a recluse, Lizzie felt it her duty to draw the Hawthornes into social interaction and offered an invitation for them to come visit.

Upon the first visit of the three Hawthorne siblings to the Peabody home, Sophia was in her room ill with a headache. Since the age of twelve, Sophia was considered an invalid by the family due to her violent headaches and was much petted and protected. Lizzie Peabody hurried upstairs to Sophia's chamber after the guests had arrived and encouraged her sister to dress and come down to join them. Referring to Hawthorne, Lizzie said, "[Y]ou never saw anything so splendid as he is—he is handsomer than Lord Byron!" [Van Doren 50]. Sophia only laughed, saying if he visited once he would come again. And she was right.

Through the ensuing months, social interaction between the two families grew. Meanwhile, Hawthorne fostered an interest in Mary Silsbee, a wealthy lady from Salem's upper social ranks. While Mary was known to be cunning and ruthless, Hawthorne, being uneducated in the wiles of women, did not recognize the danger. She appealed to the gallantry in Hawthorne, making him believe that her honor had been trampled on by a man named John Louis O'Sullivan. The conniving Mary then asked Hawthorne to champion her cause. Thinking he loved her, and not wanting to call his beloved a liar, Hawthorne recklessly challenged O'Sullivan to a duel. Thankfully, O'Sullivan handled the situation with wisdom, writing a letter to Hawthorne, explaining the truth of the matter and proving his own innocence. Not only did he refuse the challenge, O'Sullivan called upon Hawthorne to renew their existing friendship. Hawthorne did as O'Sullivan asked and at the same time severed his relationship with Mary Silsbee.

Another duel, which closely affected Hawthorne, did not have such a happy ending. In February 1838, his college friend, Jonathan Cilley, now a congressman in Washington, D.C., accepted a challenge for a political duel and was killed. The horrid affair greatly upset Hawthorne. He had visited with Cilley only a few months earlier and their friendship had grown steadily since college days. Now his friend was gone because of a foolish duel.

Through the beginning of the year 1838, Lizzie Peabody persisted in her attempts to bring Nathaniel Hawthorne out into society. She regularly sent flowers, books, and notes to the Hawthorne home. Invitations to Ebe and Louisa to go for walks often included an added note at the bottom: "Don't forget to ask your brother" [Turner 109]. If the weather proved fair and sunny, Sophia also joined them. In April, Lizzie traveled to West Newton to stay with her brother through the summer. In her letters to Sophia, she often spoke admirably of Hawthorne.

Because Sophia was considered an invalid, it was presumed she would never marry. Since she did not have the strength to be a wife and mother, she would be considered a burden to any man during that time period. Despite her health, Hawthorne was quite taken with Sophia and paid her more attention. In Lizzie's absence, Hawthorne and Sophia began spending more time together. At the time, Sophia saw herself merely as an assistant in Lizzie's scheme to draw Hawthorne out. One day when Hawthorne came to call in the afternoon rather than the evening, Sophia was quite pleased. In a letter to Lizzie, she exclaimed, "Only think what progress! To come and propose a walk at mid-day!" [Turner 110].

In later years, Elizabeth Peabody would make it seem as though she were the one who brought Hawthorne and Sophia together, when in fact her letters reveal that she was openly disappointed as she saw his intentions turning toward the younger sister. Lizzie was interested in furthering Hawthorne's literary career, but she appeared to be romantically interested in him as well. There were, in fact, rumors that Hawthorne was engaged to Elizabeth first; however, nothing has been found to support such rumors. Hawthorne's sentiments toward the eldest Peabody daughter were of gratitude and great admiration; yet, he wearied of her habit of taking command and telling others what to do. Her overbearing personality would not have been a good fit for the sensitive author.

Sophia's personality, on the other hand, was generally good-natured and full of sweetness, something of a miracle given the trials she had experienced in her young life. When the wretched headaches first came on in her early teen years, her mother was convinced they developed because she had been unhappy during her pregnancy with Sophia. Dr. Peabody blamed the headaches on the drugs he himself had given to his daughter during her teething time. Whatever the cause—the malady may have been allergy-related—the family was intent on finding a cure, some of which included such drastic measures as hypnosis, arsenic, morphine, a diet of white bread and water, and even the administration of leeches, which were applied to draw blood. When the headaches developed, even the sounds of the clanking of silverware at the dinner table became unbearable. The only respite she found was to remain in a quiet, darkened room lying perfectly still.

The one thing that did seem to improve Sophia's health was time spent away from home, in spite of the fact that her unhappy mother dreaded letting Sophia out of her sight. A letter from Sophia in 1824 during a visit to her uncle's home in New Hampshire indicates she had a delightful time. She ran and played, and even hiked up a mountain without feeling fatigued or ill. Again in 1827, visiting an aunt in Vermont, she went horseback riding and attended parties. The more she wrote home about the good time she was having, the quicker Mrs. Peabody would write back to remind Sophia of her delicate condition and urge her to return home soon. In one such letter, Mrs. Peabody wrote, "Besides, I must acknowledge, that the kind and cheering tones of your voice and your mirth-inspiring laugh, and affectionate smile would be cordial to me." She went on to warn her daughter that excitement was not good for her head: "You enjoy too fervently for your strength. Come home now and live awhile upon the past" [Gaeddert 51]. The truth was that Mrs. Peabody did not want to let Sophia go.

Elizabeth and Mary took positions as teachers and governesses. Together they opened a school in Boston, which became quite successful. Sophia lived with her sisters and helped with the school for a time, but her talent lay more in art. Elizabeth saw to it that her sister, whom she adored, received the best instruction. Each of her instructors had nothing but praise for her work. Copying art was a lucrative profession during the early 1800s, a practice that allowed wealthy families to obtain reproductions of famous artists to hang in their homes.

For a short time, Sophia made a valiant effort to live alone and support herself with her painting. Discouraged, she was soon forced to return home to Salem.

In 1833, when Sophia was twenty-four, she grew very ill. The doctors advised sending her to a warmer climate. Enterprising Lizzie found a governess position for Mary in Cuba at the home of a wealthy coffee planter. Sophia would be allowed to accompany her sister and become a guest at the home. Mary, who was in love and hoping to marry widower Horace Mann (and later did so), was reluctant to leave home, but Lizzie insisted. While in Cuba, Sophia went horseback riding each day and enjoyed a healthy diet, including oranges from the nearby groves. She spent her time painting portraits and helping entertain the children. At one of their many social events she even tried out the new dance known as the "waltz." Never had she felt better in her life. The multitude of letters from Sophia to the family (almost one per day) were gathered up and bound as the *Cuba Journals.* While her headaches never entirely went away, the improvement in Sophia's overall health was remarkable.

Upon her return to Salem the next spring, Sophia hoped the state of good health would continue, but it did not. She was once again fawned over by her mother, who saw to it that she was protected from any exertion, determined to keep Sophia in a state of eternal childhood. During the summer of 1838, however, with Lizzie away in West Newton, Sophia often came down from her room when she knew Hawthorne had come to call. She wrote to her sister, "I came down to catch a glimpse of him—He has a celestial expression which I do not like to lose. It is a manifestation of the divine in human" [Gaeddert 73].

Once when Hawthorne left Salem for a short visit to the Berkshires, Sophia reread his story, "The Gentle Boy," and then sketched a drawing of the story's hero, Ilbrahim. Showing the sketch to Hawthorne when he returned, she wanted to know if it looked like "your Ilbrahim." Hawthorne replied, "He will never look otherwise to me" [Gaeddert 74]. When the new edition of the story came out in a small book for children, it featured Sophia's drawing and a dedication to her by Hawthorne and a preface praising her work. By fall and early winter the two were taking long walks together without the accompanying sisters. While they pledged their love to one another, each felt marriage was out of the question—Sophia because of the burden of her bad health and Hawthorne because of his lack of adequate income to support a wife.

Realizing that Hawthorne needed a steady income, as well as time in which to write, Lizzie set about to find employment for him through her political contacts. Hawthorne's friends, Bridge and Pierce, pursued the same objective. Out of several appointments that were discussed and considered, the inspector's position at the Boston Custom House was the one that came through for Hawthorne. He packed up and moved to Boston to report for work in January of 1839.

Other than working in the office of his brother's stage line, this was the first non-literary job Hawthorne had ever held. His job was to count the tubs of coal or other products on board the ships. In an entry in his diary, Hawthorne described the cabin of a ship as "the rudest and dirtiest hole imaginable" [Turner 119]. Four entries in his journal are the only notebook accounts Hawthorne kept during his two years in the Boston Custom-house. He soon realized he was in an occupation that was "so alien to literature," that it was impossible to do any writing at all [Turner 119].

Most of Hawthorne's writing during this time consisted of love letters to Sophia. As the year progressed he was more ardent in his admiration toward her. She came to Boston for a time to see about the engraving made of the character Ilbrahim in "The Gentle Boy." She lodged with the family of Samuel Hooper where Hawthorne often came to call. One afternoon he came to escort her to a social outing. They never made it to their destination; instead, the two of them strolled around Boston Common and watched the sunset.

After Sophia returned to Salem, Hawthorne wrote to encourage her in her health:

> ... do be strong, and full of life—earthly life—and let there be a glow in your cheeks. And sleep soundly the whole night long, and get up every morning with a feeling as if you were newly created; and I pray you to lay up a stock of fresh energy every day till we meet again; so that we may walk miles and miles ..." [Turner 121].

By summer, he was referring to her in his letters as his wife: "Oh my dearest, how that thought thrills me! We *are* married! I felt it long ago; and sometimes, when I was seeking for some fondest word, it has been on my lips to call you—'Wife'!" [Mellow 164]. They kept their love for one another private, never publicly announcing their intentions to be married. Sophia's health also improved during their courtship.

In the summer of 1840, Sophia's sister Elizabeth moved to Boston permanently and opened a bookstore. The shop eventually became a center for the intellectual and cultural life of the city. Lizzie also dabbled in the publishing business, printing tracts and smaller books, and doing projects for the Anti-Slavery Society. Sophia lived in an upstairs studio room where she did her paintings, some of which were displayed for sale in the store.

After two years of working in the Boston Custom House, Hawthorne tendered his resignation. He had, it seemed, found the answer for a place where he could write freely and also make a home for his fiancée. The place was a working commune known as Brook Farm.

## THE OLD MANSE

Within Elizabeth Peabody's circle of influential friends was a minister named George Ripley. Ripley was promoting a plan for an ideal community combining laborers and intellectuals. The experiment would take place on a dairy farm known as Brook Farm in West Roxbury. Lizzie enthusiastically promoted the project, relaying the information to Hawthorne. He, in turn, warmed to the idea because he wearied of politics and longed to return to his writing. On the surface, Brook Farm seemed to be the answer, prompting him to sink $1,000 of his savings into the venture.

Early letters from Hawthorne at Brook Farm were enthusiastic, boasting of the cows he had milked, the wood he had cut, and the other farm chores he had completed. Soon however, Hawthorne saw that he was doing much more than his share of the work, and his writing time was as far removed from him as it had been at the Custom House.

In a letter to his sister, Louisa, he said he was certain he would make a "complete" farmer. She, however, doubted that fact, as did his mother and Ebe. "I do not like your working so hard at all," Louisa wrote. "... I cannot bear to think that this hot sun is beating upon your head. You could but work hard if you could do nothing else; as it is, you can do a great deal better. What is the use of burning your brains out in the sun, when you can do anything better with them?" [Van Doren 112].

The original plan was for each person at the farm to work three or four hours per day, which would have left ample time for his writing. In reality, Hawthorne was working every day from dawn until dusk. By summer, he wrote to Sophia, "Thou and I must form other plans for ourselves, for I can see few or no signs that Providence purposes to give us a home here. I am weary, weary, thrice weary of waiting so many ages" [Mellow 187]. The "waiting" he mentioned referred to marrying his beloved. Even though his savings were gone, Hawthorne made plans for the wedding to take place by the summer of 1841. Returning to his "chamber under the eaves" in Salem, he wrote with a flourish; turning out a number of stories—his family was pleased to have him home once again.

That Hawthorne was doted upon and adored by his mother and sisters would be an understatement—he was the center of their lives. Therefore, he was unsure how to inform them of his upcoming marriage. Not only would he be giving himself to his bride, but he would be leaving Salem as well. With the wedding set to take place in June, he told his sisters in May and his mother in June. While his sisters were somewhat reserved about the idea, his mother was entirely receptive. In a letter to Sophia on June 9, he wrote, "Foolish me, to doubt that my mother's love would be wise, like all other genuine love.... It seems that our mother had seen how things were, a long time ago.... My sisters, too, begin to sympathize as they ought; and all is well" [Mellow 196]. All was well, except for a last-minute case of nerves on Sophia's part, causing the date to be postponed another week. The ceremony took place July 9 in the parlor of Dr. Peabody's home at 13 West Street, Boston. Only a few friends and family members were in attendance. Hawthorne's sisters did not attend. Directly following the ceremony, the couple left in a carriage to travel to their new home in Concord, Massachusetts.

The house in which they lived was an old parsonage built in 1770 for the Reverend William Emerson. Situated close by the Concord River, the "Old Manse," as Hawthorne came to call it, already had a rich heritage. From his study window, Reverend Emerson watched the battle at the North Bridge that sent British troops scurrying in April 1775. Emerson volunteered as chaplain for the patriots and died of fever before the war was over. Reverend Ezra Ripley then acquired the property and married Emerson's widow. Ripley laid out extensive orchards, which he lived to enjoy until his death at age ninety. Added to these were vegetable gardens and current bushes of which the newlywed Hawthornes would reap the harvests. The place had a sense of remoteness about it, enhanced by borders of thick trees.

Because of Sophia's mother's concern for her daughter's health, an Irish cook, Molly Bryan, had been hired to assist the young bride. Molly was waiting for them at the Old Manse when they arrived. Since the house was rented furnished, little was required in order to move in. Hawthorne's books and papers and their few pieces of furniture had been sent ahead of them. In this idyllic environment, the couple settled into a quiet, romantic existence. They jointly kept an ongoing journal of their married life. These entries, as well as the letters written by Sophia to her mother, revealed how happy they were together. "It is four weeks tomorrow since we came," she wrote, "and it seems at the same time one moment and a thousand years" [Mellow 204].

After all Hawthorne's backbreaking work at Brook Farm to coax plants to grow in the rocky soil, he was delighted with the abundant harvest that came in late summer. A peach tree just outside the kitchen window was so heavy with fruit that he had to prop up the branches. "I feel somewhat overwhelmed with the impending bounties of Providence," he wrote in his journal [Mellow 207].

Among their close neighbors were such literary notables as Margaret Fuller, Ralph Waldo Emerson, Bronson Alcott (father of author, Louisa May Alcott) and Henry David Thoreau. Hawthorne purchased the canoe which Thoreau and his brother had made. Hawthorne learned to maneuver the craft with oars, but never succeeded in paddling it in the steady way that Thoreau did. While the Hawthornes enjoyed receiving visitors, they were most happy when left totally alone. "My wife is, in the strictest sense, my sole companion," he wrote in their journal, "and I need no other—there is no vacancy in my mind, any more than in my heart" [Mellow 217]. While his life had been made up of solitude, Sophia's had not. In spite of her illness, she had always been surrounded by friends and family. Hawthorne marveled that she could be as content as he in their quiet aloneness, especially during the long winter, which was unusually harsh that year.

Being so happy and contented took a toll on Hawthorne's writing. He found it difficult to shut himself away and concentrate on his work. At times, Sophia had to order him to go to his study and remain there for a suitable amount of time; however, they both enjoyed fun outdoors.

Ice skating was a particular joy for Hawthorne because, he admitted, it made him feel like a little boy again. In their exuberance, however, Sophia took a bad fall and, being a few months pregnant, suffered a miscarriage. While they were deeply grieved over the incident, they were confident other children would be forthcoming. "God will surely crown our union with children," Hawthorne wrote, "because it fulfills the highest conditions of marriage" [Mellow 220].

Funds for the newlyweds were in short supply during their early years together. While Hawthorne was selling his work—over twenty published pieces during his stay at the Manse—publications were slow to pay, stifling his cash flow. This never-ending problem plagued and frustrated him. As he waited for money owed him, Hawthorne fell behind in his payments to the local merchants. "The system of slack payment in this country," he said in a letter to Horatio Bridge, "is most abominable ..." [Mellow 226]. Bridge, who had been appointed purser on the U.S.S. *Saratoga*, was bound for a two-year voyage at sea. Hawthorne encouraged Bridge to write about his journey after which Hawthorne would edit the works with the idea of having them published. In the resulting book, published under the title, *Journal of an African Cruiser*, Hawthorne was listed as the editor and received a small part of the royalties. The book received generous attention and praise in England.

With the coming of spring, Sophia was pregnant again, and now Hawthorne was convinced his writing could not support a growing family. Much as he hated the thought, Hawthorne would have to secure a reliable income. Many new periodicals, in which his works were published, failed after only a few issues, making him wary of submitting at all.

On March 3, 1844, their daughter, Una, came into the world. Sophia's mother was on hand to assist with the delivery. In letters to his family Hawthorne expressed his great joy over the event. To Bridge, he said, "If you want a new feeling in this weary life, get married, and make yourself a father. It renews the world from the surface to the center" [Mellow 240]. To friend, George Hillard, he sounded a more somber tone. Hawthorne noted that after such an event as the birth of a child "the spirit never can be thoroughly gay and careless again." He confessed he'd been a "trifler" for a long time and must become more serious. "I have business on earth now, and must look about me for the means of doing it." In order to make a living, he considered writing what he called literary drudgery: "translation, concocting of school-books, newspaper-scribbling, etc." [Mellow 240]. Una's arrival changed a good many things, not the least of which was the attitude of Hawthorne's own mother. Hawthorne, Sophia, and the baby spent Thanksgiving week in the Hawthorne home, and for the first time that he could remember, his mother dined with the family—holding Una on her lap.

Finances, or lack thereof, continued to press the Hawthornes. They reluctantly let Molly go, after which, as Sophia told in her letters, Hawthorne arose early each morning to set the fire and start breakfast. Sophia diligently patched her husband's worn-out clothes, and they retired early in the evening to conserve oil for the lamps. Hawthorne indicated in his journals that being short of funds did not disturb him nearly as much as being owed money that was not paid.

The 1845 elections brought the Democrats back into office, which meant that several of Hawthorne's friends were intently trying to find a political appointment for him. When Bridge returned from his African excursion, he came to Concord for a visit, bringing Pierce with him. When they arrived, Hawthorne was out in the shed cutting wood. Sophia recalled that when the three men emerged from the shed after a long conversation, "Mr. Pierce's arm was encircling my husband's old blue frock. How his friends do love him!" [Van Doren 134]. Among other things discussed in the woodshed was the vacancy of the surveyorship at the Salem Custom-house. Hawthorne could obtain the position, but he would need to become better known in certain circles in the Salem community. In order to facilitate community relations, Bridge invited the Hawthornes to come to his home in the Navy Yard near Portsmouth, New Hampshire. He also invited several key senators including Senator and Mrs. Pierce. All the guests dined together and spent time on boating and fishing excursions. Hawthorne must have made a good impression because his appointment was forthcoming.

Meanwhile, a minister from Concord, Reverend Charles Upham, moved to Salem and began spreading rumors about the Hawthornes' dire financial straits. In his telling, their situation was hopeless and a political appointment was all that stood between them and the poor house. It was not the last time that Upham would cause problems for Hawthorne. Before the appointment could be completely secured, news came that the owner of the Old Manse, Samuel Ripley, wanted to move back in. The place was to be vacated by early October. Even before they left, carpenters had arrived to begin renovations, many of which saddened Hawthorne. Still lacking adequate funds, he moved his little family back to the Hawthorne family house in Salem, where it was hoped they would only have to stay a short while.

"We gathered up our household goods," he wrote regarding their last day in Eden, "drank a farewell cup of tea in our pleasant little breakfast-room ... and passed forth between the tall stone gate-posts, as uncertain as the wandering Arabs where our tent might next be pitched" [Mellow 265].

## THE FAMED AUTHOR

The move to Herbert Street took place in early October 1845, and the stay stretched throughout the winter. Hawthorne had dubbed his childhood home, "Castle Dismal," because his mother and two sisters had lived there in near seclusion. The old house was quite cold, and Sophia worried about Una being on the icy floors. If living with in-laws were not precarious enough, they learned that another baby was on the way. And still they had no official word on an appointment for Hawthorne. Meanwhile, he returned to the chamber beneath the eaves where, as he put it, he had wasted so many years of his youth. There, in the midst of the uncertainty, Hawthorne struggled to put the finishing touches on his book, *Mosses from an Old Manse*. This collection of sketches and short stories was based on their experiences living in Concord.

In March 1846 they decided that Sophia would live in Boston to be near her doctor until the baby arrived. Since the Horace Manns (Sophia's sister Mary was Horace Mann's wife) would be leaving to go to West Newton, the Hawthornes were invited to live temporarily in their vacated house. Being in Boston appealed to Sophia, who felt Salem was a social vacuum. Shortly after their decision was made, on March 23, Hawthorne at last received his appointment as surveyor of the Custom House in Salem. This job, and the circumstances that surrounded it, would be the catalyst to launch him into writing *The Scarlet Letter*, bringing him into the literary spotlight.

The news of the appointment buoyed Hawthorne's confidence and he was able to finish his essay, which was to be a preface for *Mosses from an Old Manse.* He asked his publishers, Wiley and Putnam, to have specially bound copies sent to a number of his friends, one of whom was Miss Charlotte Marshall, soon to be married to his friend, Horatio Bridge. The book met with a number of favorable reviews.

During the summer months spent in Boston, Hawthorne worked hard at his job as surveyor, taking the train each day from Boston to Salem and back again. In the course of his work as surveyor, Hawthorne applied his official stamp on crates and bags that traveled around the globe—"N. Hawthorne, Sur'$^r$." He was amused that his name should experience such a "queer vehicle of fame" after he had authored a book of short stories as well as numerous articles [Mellow 272]. His post as surveyor had pulled him out of a comfortable circle of literary friends in Concord, to a setting where no one had heard of him nor read his works.

Early in the summer, Hawthorne's son Julian was born. Writing to his sister, Louisa, Hawthorne had this to say of Julian's arrival on June 22: "A small troglodyte made his appearance here at ten minutes to six o'clock this morning, who claimed to be your nephew, and the heir to all our wealth and honors" [Mellow 273]. For a time, they lived in a small house on Chestnut Street, which was too cramped to give Hawthorne his own study. After they moved to the larger house on Mall Street and Madame Hawthorne and the two spinster sisters joined them, life settled into a routine. Hawthorne's family was his greatest delight during the Salem years. Daily logs tell in great detail of the bright sayings and silly antics of his two children.

In his study in the Mall Street House he wrote regularly, completing several tales and sketches but without the freedom he'd experienced previously. "At last by main strength, I have wrenched and torn an idea out of my miserable brain," he wrote to one editor, "or rather, the fragment of an idea, like a tooth ill-drawn, and leaving the roots to torture me" [Van Doren 138]. To enhance his literary life, he took the position of manager and corresponding secretary of the Salem Lyceum. His job entailed scheduling lecturers, many of whom were his old friends from Concord. Thoreau came on two occasions and stayed at the Mall Street house each time. Other speakers were Emerson, Bronson Alcott, Daniel Webster, and publisher, James T. Fields.

The first rumblings of discontent against Hawthorne as the Salem surveyor were done in secret, mostly led by Charles Upham, who seemed intent on spreading rumors about him. At the time when the official word arrived of his removal from office, Hawthorne was much more concerned about his children, who had both contracted scarlet fever. In a letter to Longfellow he commented in regards to the children, "Other troubles may irritate me superficially; nothing else can go near the heart" [Mellow 294].

In 1849, a heated political whirlwind involving slurs and accusations left Hawthorne and his wife feeling betrayed by their own town. Both vacillated between the desire to have Hawthorne vindicated and the desire to be rid of the despised political position. To make matters worse, Hawthorne's mother became gravely ill and by July lay on her deathbed attended by her daughters, as well as Hawthorne and Sophia. Hawthorne and his mother had never been particularly close, but one day while visiting the sickroom, he knelt by her bedside, grasped her weak hand, and collapsed into sobs of grief. In his journal he noted, "... surely it is the darkest hour I ever lived" [Mellow 297]. She died late in the afternoon of July 31, 1849.

As the political turmoil came to a head, Hawthorne ceased to try to retain the position, but did make an attempt to assure the public that he had been removed on false or insufficient grounds. However, regarding the perpetrator of most of the rumors, Charles Upham, the usually mild-mannered Hawthorne stated in a letter, "... if Mr. Upham should give me occasion—or perhaps if he should not—I shall do my best to kill and scalp him in the public prints; and I think I shall succeed." [Turner, pg. 186] In later years, Hawthorne found he could freely forgive Upham for the damages he caused. Although losing his job was a bitter blow, Hawthorne was sure that if he had stayed at the Custom House four years longer he would "have rusted utterly away" [Turner 199].

After the political furor over the dismissal died down, both Hawthorne and Sophia were inwardly relieved at the final outcome. For it was after his dismissal and after the death of his mother that Hawthorne threw himself into writing *The Scarlet Letter*. In September Sophia wrote to her mother, "Mr. Hawthorne writes immensely. I am almost frightened about it. But he is well now, and looks very shining" [Hawthorne J. 353-4].

During the winter of 1849–50, while Hawthorne was writing the novel, he received a visit from James Fields. The two men had first met when Hawthorne invited Fields to lecture at the Salem Lyceum. Fields paid a visit to the Mall Street house because he'd heard that Hawthorne was ill. During their conversation, Fields pressed Hawthorne to reveal what he had been writing. Always private and quiet, the author was hesitant to tell. However, Fields persisted in his request. Before he left the house, Fields had in his hands the draft of the manuscript for *The Scarlet Letter.* Reading it in the train on the way home, Fields was so impressed that he immediately arranged for the work to printed by his publishing house.

Fields had joined with William D. Ticknor to form the publishing company of Ticknor & Fields. The two would later publish the works of world-renowned author, Charles Dickens. Both men took good care of their writers, which Hawthorne could not help but appreciate after the sour experiences he had had with publishing houses. This publisher-writer relationship would be solid and long-lasting.

When Hawthorne finished the book in February of 1850, both his publisher and his wife raved about it. When he read the last chapter to Sophia, she wept. "It broke her heart," he said, "and sent her to bed with a grievous headache—which I look upon as a triumphant success! Judging from its effect on her and the publisher, I may calculate on what bowlers call a ten-strike!" [Turner 193]. The book came out in March, and the first edition of 2,500 copies sold out in ten days. A second run of 3,000 also quickly sold out. Some of its appeal was due in part to the extensive publicity Hawthorne had received from his Custom-house ousting. The book was in every way a success, even financially.

During the latter part of 1849, funds for the Hawthornes had been almost nonexistent. Friends who knew their plight had helped out by loaning Hawthorne money, all of which he eventually repaid. But with the success of *The Scarlet Letter,* he now had the means by which to move far from Salem. "I detest this town so much," he wrote to Bridge, "that I hate to go into the streets, or to have the people see me. Anywhere else, I shall at once be entirely another man" [Turner 208-9].

While Hawthorne had a deep love for the sea, he thought perhaps the Berkshire Mountains in western Massachusetts might be better for the family's overall health. Making a visit to Lenox—just over the line from Stockbridge—they found a little red house which proved suitable and made preparations to move. Sending their belongings ahead, the Hawthorne family went by train on May 23. Friends offered the house rent-free, but Hawthorne insisted on paying fifty dollars a year. He immediately set about planting a vegetable garden big enough to feed all of Salem. The eight-room house was no beauty, but it was their first time to be alone as a family since they left Concord. Hawthorne called it the "ugliest little old red farm-house," which he added was "as red as the Scarlet Letter" [Turner 210].

Sophia's joy knew no bounds and her letters rejoice over every detail of the house, her decorations, and the placement of furniture. Lenox offered a beautiful lake surrounded by wooded hills and craggy mountains. The family spent time together working in the garden, walking in the meadows, bathing in the lake, cutting wood, sledding, and ice skating. Nathaniel Hawthorne seemed never to tire of playing with his children. A steady stream of visitors came and went, but Hawthorne was not always reciprocal in social interaction. For the most part, Hawthorne still guarded his privacy and his quiet time and preferred to be with his own family than with any friends.

A new twist to his growing fame was a steady stream of letters and small gifts from the appreciative readers of *The Scarlet Letter*. None went unanswered. Author Herman Melville, who had recently moved to the area, was one of the persons with whom Hawthorne chose to spend quality time. The two were at crucial points in their respective careers and their relationship provided the support each needed.

In spite of the torrid heat of summer—Hawthorne was accustomed to cool sea breezes—he was hard at work on another novel entitled, *The House of the Seven Gables*. The work went well but slower than *The Scarlet Letter*. Since summer was not his usual time to write, Hawthorne struggled against gazing out the window of his study. This book, he noted, required more care and thought. It would not be finished until the following January.

The winter proved blissful, especially after Sophia learned she was once again pregnant. She taught the children throughout the day, letting them play outside in the cold for short periods of time. When their father came down from his study, there was great rejoicing. After the children were put to bed, Hawthorne read aloud to his wife, who claimed his reading was better than any stage acting she had ever seen.

*The House of the Seven Gables* was also an instant success, bringing Hawthorne more clearly into public view. Reviews of the book were favorable in both the United States and England. Two printings came out in April, a third in May, and a fourth in September, from which Hawthorne made fifteen percent royalties on each dollar for which the book sold.

In the second summer at Lenox, he completed a series of children's stories entitled *A Wonder-Book*. In spite of the fact that he disliked writing in the summer, Hawthorne rushed to comply with Fields' assertive public relations program. Once the manuscript was sent off in mid-July, Hawthorne wrote, "I am going to begin to enjoy the summer now and to read foolish novels, if I can get any, and smoke cigars and think of nothing at all—which is equivalent to thinking of all manner of things" [Mellow 369]. That same year, on May 20, Rose Hawthorne was born and her arrival made the little, red house even more crowded. As the summer advanced, the heat of the Berkshires became almost unbearable for all of them. "This is a horrible, horrible, most hor-r-ible climate," he wrote in his journal, "... I detest it! I detest it!! I detest it!!! I hate Berkshire with my whole soul, and would joyfully see its mountains laid flat" [Mellow 376]. From that point on, Hawthorne looked for an opportunity to move away from Lenox.

In July, Sophia took the girls to visit her family, all of whom had moved from Boston to West Newton. During their absence, Hawthorne was left behind with Julian, along with the cook, Mrs. Peters, and Bunny, the new pet rabbit. Hawthorne's thoughts of spending a few quiet days were quickly set aside as he entertained the lively Julian, who talked non-stop. Throughout the three weeks that the ladies were away, Hawthorne kept a detailed journal, which is both warm and humorous. Reflecting on a particular walk, Hawthorne wrote that Julian "was never out of spirits, and is certainly as happy as the day is long. He is happy enough by himself; and when I sympathize, or partake in his play, it is almost too much, and he nearly explodes with laughter and delight" [Hawthorne, J. 414]. The days of separation were long until the family was reunited in late August.

In September, Hawthorne made a trip to Salem. On the way, he stopped in West Newton to visit Sophia's sister, Mary, and her husband, Horace Mann, who had recently been elected to Congress. Since the Manns would be moving to Washington, D.C., they offered to rent their house to the Hawthornes for the winter. As quickly as that, the question of moving from Lenox was settled. Julian would later remember their day of departure from the little red house:

On the 21st of November, 1851, the family with their trunks, got into a large farmer's wagon, and were driven to Pittsfield, leaving the little red house empty behind them. It was a bleak day; and one of the party remembers that the five cats which had been fellow inmates for many months, driven by some inscrutable instinct that this departure was final ... evacuated the premises in a body, and scampered after the wagon for about a quarter of a mile. [Hawthorne, J. 429-39]

West Newton in winter, Julian would also remember, was dismal and unlovely—a stark contrast to the beautiful wooded hills around Lenox.

## CONSUL TO LIVERPOOL

The Hawthornes considered West Newton, like Lenox, to be temporary from the outset of their move. However, Hawthorne was able to write, and from December to April he completed his third major work, *The Blithedale Romance*. Published on July 14, the book used many of Hawthorne's observations from Brook Farm, where he had lived ten years earlier. Fields sold *The Blithedale Romance* to a British publisher for two hundred pounds, the first payment he had ever received for works published abroad. Nathaniel Hawthorne, now considered by many as a literary genius, saw favorable reviews of the newest work. *The Blithedale Romance*, however, experienced a more short-lived popularity in comparison to his former works.

Shortly after their arrival in West Newton, they learned that the Alcott house in Concord was for sale. Upon his inspection of the place in February, Hawthorne purchased the house and nine acres of land for $1,500. Additional acres were purchased later. It would be the first home they ever owned. Sophia and the girls went ahead in early June to set the house in order, with Hawthorne and Julian joining them a week later. The house, in which author, Louisa May Alcott grew up, was originally called "Hillside" by Bronson Alcott. Hawthorne changed the name to "The Wayside."

The old farmhouse, built before the Revolutionary War, had been added onto by Alcott and provided spacious quarters for the Hawthornes with three growing children. It was located only three-quarters of a mile from Emerson's home and two miles from the Old Manse, which still held pleasant memories for both Hawthorne and Sophia. Since their marriage, they had lived in seven different houses, and Hawthorne later said that the Wayside was the first in which he truly felt at home.

On the same day the Hawthornes moved into their new home, the Democratic Party convened in Baltimore to choose their candidate for President. In the steamy heat, the fragmented party went through ballot after ballot with no results. For five days the balloting continued until finally on the thirty-first ballot, Hawthorne's college friend, Franklin Pierce, received the presidential nomination. Once he heard the news, Hawthorne wrote his congratulations and offered to write a campaign biography for his friend. Ticknor & Fields agreed to be the publisher. Writing for Pierce would not be the most popular venture for Hawthorne, since most of his Concord friends were liberalists. Even his own brother-in-law Horace Mann, not an admirer of Pierce, had remarked that if Hawthorne succeeded in making a hero out of such a lackluster figure as Pierce, it would be "the greatest work of fiction he ever wrote" [Mellow 408]. As abolitionists became more and more outspoken against slavery, the nation grew more deeply divided. As a result, politics turned bitter and rancorous. Many rumors about Pierce—most untrue—were spread and then dogged him most of his life. Such slander grieved both Hawthorne and Sophia, who counted Pierce as a dear, close friend; yet, family matters soon redirected the Hawthornes' grief.

After the Hawthornes left Salem in 1850, the extended family household on Mall Street was of necessity, broken up, leaving Ebe to make her home with a farming family on the seacoast outside of Salem. There she lived in quiet contentment for many years, still healthy and alert into old age. While on occasion, Louisa might visit Hawthorne's home, Ebe never ventured further from her house than she could walk. After moving from Lenox to Concord, Hawthorne and Sophia encouraged Louisa to come and visit. She had accepted, but kept putting it off due to other commitments.

In July, Sophia received a note from Louisa from Sarasota Springs where she had gone with her uncle, John Dike. He had traveled there to take the spa waters for his health. On July 26 they boarded the steamboat, *Henry Clay* to return to Salem by way of the Hudson River and New York City. Just off the Palisades, near Fort Lee, New Jersey, fire broke out on board. Louisa had been in her cabin reading *Pilgrim's*

*Progress.* Her uncle spoke with her only a short time before the fire broke out, after which he had returned to the upper deck. Dike was rescued, but Louisa died. Sophia would later state in a letter to her mother that they did not know if Louisa died by fire, or if she had drowned. Word was brought to the Hawthornes by way of family friend, William Pike. Hawthorne immediately shut himself up in his study to mourn the loss of his dear sister. He traveled back to Salem but arrived too late for the funeral service. Louisa was buried in the family plot at the Howard Street Cemetery where Madame Hawthorne, Louisa's Manning grandparents, and other Manning family members were buried.

Grieving the death of his sister pulled Hawthorne away from the work at hand for only a short time. The manuscript of the Pierce biography was delivered to Ticknor & Fields in late August, after which Hawthorne instructed his publishers to push the book hard. "We are politicians now," he noted in his letter, "and you must not expect to conduct yourself like a gentlemanly publisher" [Mellow 414]. This statement shows that Hawthorne was contemplating the acceptance of a position from Pierce, should he become President. In a letter to Bridge, Hawthorne was more open: "A foreign mission I could not afford to take," he wrote. "The consulship at Liverpool, I might; and he could not do a better thing, either for me or the credit of his administration than to make the appointment" [Mellow 414-5]. Nathaniel Hawthorne's fame had spread throughout England and the idea of living there as an honored official at the expense of the United States government was an appealing one, to say nothing of the steady income.

Pierce won the electoral vote, but the popular vote was weak, which further undermined the confidence of the people in their new President. As a leader who ruled over a divided party and a divided nation, Pierce found himself overwhelmed by a series of circumstances of which he had little or no control. On January 6, as Pierce, his wife Jane, and their only child, Benjamin, were traveling from Boston to Concord, New Hampshire, the train car in which they were riding toppled over and careened down an embankment. While the president-elect and his wife escaped without harm, their eleven-year-old son was killed instantly. Years earlier, the couple had lost a son in childbirth, and yet another son to typhus at the age of five. Benny was their last remaining child.

Jane had never wanted her husband to run for the office of president, now her grief was almost more than she could bear. She did not accompany her husband to the inauguration ceremonies. Throughout his tenure she remained mostly secluded, writing notes to her dead son.

As soon as Pierce was in office, Hawthorne's friends turned to him as a contact when seeking political offices from the President. Even the wife of his friend Horatio Bridge wrote to him asking if he could arrange an important administrative post for her husband. Some seekers, such as Herman Melville, Hawthorne attempted to help, but others he simply turned away.

Prior to the inauguration, Sophia's mother, Mrs. Peabody grew gravely ill. Mary and Lizzie wrote to Sophia insisting that she not try to travel to Boston because the children needed her at home. Mrs. Peabody died on January 11, 1853. Amidst these continuing distractions, Hawthorne began writing a sequel to his collection of children's stories, a book he would entitle *Tanglewood Tales*. He derived much joy from the project. "I never did anything else so well as these old baby stories," he wrote to a friend [Mellow 422].

Word of Hawthorne's appointment to the Liverpool Consul arrived in March, after which he made a trip to Washington, D.C. in April to officially accept the position. He was accompanied by his publisher and friend, William Ticknor. Yet another tragedy had struck when Pierce's Vice President, William R. King fell ill and died. Time spent at the capitol was not pleasant for Hawthorne. Pierce, still attempting to appoint his cabinet, was too distracted to spend much time with his old friend. Hawthorne and Ticknor both quickly wearied of the political intrigue; Hawthorne also disliked being in the limelight, and he received much attention as a celebrity.

After Hawthorne's return home, the family made preparations for their departure to England. Sophia's brother, Nathaniel Peabody, and his family were to live in The Wayside during the Hawthornes' absence. The family took the train to Boston on July 6, and there boarded the *Niagara*. As the ship pulled out of the harbor, a salute was fired in honor of the departure of the new consul to Liverpool. The voyage, blessed with fair weather, took ten days, landing them in Liverpool on July 16. They stayed briefly at the Waterloo Hotel until they relocated to a comfortable boardinghouse. The house, run by Mrs. Blodget, was located at 133 Duke Street and offered comfortable quarters and hearty meals.

By August 4, Hawthorne had settled into his office as consul, reviewing the books and records and beginning his four-year term. He attended to every detail with the same energy and drive that he had given at the Boston Custom House, the Salem Custom House, and Brook Farm. By the fourteenth of the month, he recorded in his journal, "Many scenes which I should have liked to record have occurred; but the pressure of business has prevented me from recording them from day to day ..." [Mellow 430].

The consul's work was demanding and important, requiring Hawthorne to become familiar with diverse matters such as quarantine regulations, examinations for licenses issued by the Marine Board, annual imports of cotton, prices of sails and sailcloth, the number of seamen shipped and discharged at the Liverpool Sailors Home, and an improved form of anchor. The job was also somewhat depressing. The consul saw his own countrymen at their worst. One of Hawthorne's first duties was to attend to the matters of an American ship captain who had died. It was Hawthorne's duty to inventory the man's effects and ship them home to the family along with a letter of condolences. He also attended the captain's funeral.

When a young American man was found in a state of insanity on the streets of a Liverpool suburb, the matter was brought to the consul's office to decide what should be done with him. The brutal cases of mistreated sailors often came to Hawthorne's attention and he had to decide under whose jurisdiction the case should fall—whether an American or a British court. The stories touched his heart, causing Hawthorne to call for the reform of laws governing the relationship between shipmasters and seamen, stating that the system needed changing.

In a letter to Senator Charles Sumner, he asked the statesman to forget about the problems of slavery for a little while and pay attention to the state of America's ships at sea. "The shipping masters in the American ports seem to be at the bottom, or near the bottom, of the mischief ..." he wrote. "[They] should be annihilated at once—no slave drivers are so wicked as they, and there is nothing in slavery so bad as the system with which they are connected" [Mellow 435]. Hawthorne sent numerous official reports to Washington, D.C. regarding these problems, but with little effect. Speaking out on issues was not in character for the quiet author. However, Hawthorne's cry for reform and justice aboard American ships was sounded until his last day in office.

If reform was a new direction in Hawthorne's life, so was the social life that his office required. His first formal affair took place a few days after his arrival when he attended a dinner at the home of the Mayor of Liverpool. He described everything as "gorgeous"—the rooms, the lighting, the plates, the dinner. Toasts were offered all around while the orchestra played American tunes (but Hawthorne did not know if it was "Hail Columbia" or "Yankee Doodle," since he did not have an ear for music). "At the conclusion," he recorded, "being cornered and with no alternative—I got upon my legs and made a response. They received me and listened to my nonsense with a good deal of rapping ... My speech was not more than two or three inches long ..." [Mellow 430]. This social event and his speech were the first of many.

Liverpool was not the best place for a family to be introduced to England, since neither the weather nor the scenery was very pleasant. Hawthorne described the Mersey River as having a "mud-puddly hue." The cold, damp, rainy weather chilled a person to the bone. In one of his journals Hawthorne stated that the city had "the very gloomiest atmosphere that ever I was acquainted with" [Mellow 433].

The monetary income also fell short of what Hawthorne had anticipated. From his salary, Hawthorne paid his family's living expenses, the salaries of employees and clerks, and he often paid from his own pocket the expenses of needy Americans. (This was no small task, since he saw it as a necessary expense of the office to take care of those who were in difficulty.) In spite of these drawbacks, Hawthorne was able to put money away, sending regular amounts home to Ticknor, who acted as his banker. In a letter to the President dated June 7, 1855, Hawthorne wrote, "To my office, when I quit it, you must appoint either a rich man or a rogue;—no poor, honest, and capable man, will think of holding it" [Turner 274].

After the first two years in England, Hawthorne made sure his family traveled to see the country, all the while lamenting that his children led a nomadic life in which they enjoyed no real home. On their first visit to London, Hawthorne saw the sights with his family in the daytime, but walked about for hours alone in the evenings, filling his notebooks with impressions and observations. There were trips to Chester, to old Boston, to Stratford-on-Avon, to Abbotsford and the Scott country. Forays into museums were particularly dreary for Hawthorne. He could never appreciate the idea of filling endless halls with old relics from the past:

I wander from hall to hall with a weary and heavy heart, wishing (Heaven forgive me!) that the Elgin Marbles and the frieze of the Parthenon were all burnt to lime.... The present is burthened too much with the past. We have not time, in our earthly existence, to appreciate what is warm with life, and immediately around us; yet we heap up all these old shells, out of which human life has long emerged, casting them off forever. I do not see how future ages are to stagger onward under all this dead weight, with the additions that will be continually made to it. [Van Doren 209]

Since the damp winters were difficult for Sophia and bad for her health, they agreed that she and the girls would travel to Lisbon, Spain for the winter. After their departure in October 1855, Hawthorne was lonely and depressed. Christmas proved to be especially difficult. By January Hawthorne confessed in his journal that he had never been in such low spirits, and all was blamed on his "desolate, bachelor condition." [Turner 290]. The family was not reunited until the following June.

Hawthorne, determined that his family would not be separated again, tendered his resignation to the newly-elected President Buchanan. It was to become effective August 31, 1857, but he was forced to stay on for six more months due to the slow process of replacement and the illness of his chief clerk. "I am weary, weary, of London and of England," he wrote in December 1857. And Liverpool had become a "black and miserable hole" [Van Doren 217]. After being relieved of his duties in October, Hawthorne moved his family to London while waiting for the accounts of the consul's office to be officially closed. The accounts were finally closed on the last day of December, and the Hawthornes left on January 5 for an extended stay on the Continent.

For five long years the novelist had served as a government official, giving all his time and effort to the task. Now it was time to return to his pen and paper.

## RETURN TO WAYSIDE

Always adversely affected by inclement weather, Hawthorne was miserable in Paris. Cold, drenching rains rendered the city black and dreary. All was made worse because he suffered from a bad cold and intermittent nosebleeds.

The Hawthornes' family group had already added a nurse for the children, now included a tutor Ada Shepard. Ada, a graduate of Antioch College where Horace Mann was president, had been chosen for the position by Mary Mann, Sophia's sister. Ada required no salary, but only needed to have her expenses paid; she remained with the family for the remainder of their stay abroad.

After a short time in France, they continued on to Rome where the weather was no better. Hawthorne's journal was filled with his loathing of the place, noting that he could not get warm. In fact, it was the worst winter in Rome in twenty years, so his laments were no exaggeration. However, when spring arrived, he became completely enraptured with Rome and Italy in general.

During their stay in Italy, Hawthorne and Sophia were surrounded by friends and acquaintances, mostly authors, artists, and sculptors. Robert and Elizabeth Browning, whom they had met in England, and William Cullen Bryant, were among the group. In the spring they traveled to Florence to spend the summer. Even the journey itself was pure joy to Hawthorne, who recorded in his journal that he had never felt so rested or serene. The American sculptor, Hiram Powers, located living quarters for the Hawthorne family in the Casa del Bello, directly across the street from his own studio. The old edifice was built around a courtyard brimming over with flowers, grass, and trees, and graced with a bubbling fountain. The entire family loved Florence at once. With balmy weather and the presence of good friends, Hawthorne found this place to be the perfect respite between his long years as a consul and his eventual return to New England. For the first time in many years, Sophia and Hawthorne enjoyed complete leisure.

By late summer a move was made to the Villa Montauto located just a mile or so outside Rome. The spacious villa offered them adventure as well as relaxation. Hawthorne enjoyed spending evenings in the tower, which overlooked the landscape and had a panoramic view of the starlit nights. He was already forming in his mind and his notes the outline for a novel—one with Italy as its setting. Hawthorne took great satisfaction in writing again. By the time they returned to Rome in October, he had completed most of a rough draft for his Italian romance.

Once again at the mercy of the weather, he complained in his journal about the "extremely spirit-crushing ... remorseless gray, with its icy heart...." [Turner 333]. Then he added that Una had taken the Roman fever, which was something akin to malaria. The next few months took a toll on the entire Hawthorne family. Una's illness grew serious and hung on for almost six months, bringing her to the point of death at least twice. Sophia stayed by her bedside almost constantly. The doctor ordered quinine to be administered in the intervals between the fever fits. Sophia's job was to keep watch and make sure it was administered properly at the correct times.

Throughout the long months, Una would begin to recover and then suffer relapses. Hawthorne was totally distraught throughout the ordeal, feeling that the shadow of misfortune must always follow the good times. He wrote little in his notebooks during her illness, but forced himself to work on the romance in progress. Friends were constantly on hand bringing flowers, gifts and food, and offering encouragement. In March, Una recovered enough to leave the house and enjoy the Roman Carnival, after which she suffered the worst relapse of all. During this nightmare period, Franklin Pierce and his wife arrived in Rome. To have his old friend by his side was particularly calming to Hawthorne. Pierce called at their home every day and sometimes twice a day. He made Hawthorne go out with him on long walks.

For the most part, Sophia's faith and optimism never wavered. However, in this last bout after long hours with no rest, she walked to the window to pray and experienced what she would call a religious transformation. In total abandonment, she turned Una over to God and trusted Him. "Why should I doubt the goodness of God?" she asked herself. "Let Him take her, if He sees best ... I will not fight against Him any more" [Mellow 512]. Returning to Una's bedside, Sophia found the fever had broken and her daughter breathing normally. From that point on, Una's health slowly but steadily improved.

By late May the family made preparations to leave Rome. Their travels to England were slow for Una's sake. By June, Hawthorne found that he experienced a strange longing for England. Upon learning that his friend and publisher, James Fields was in England with his new wife (his first wife had died in 1851), Hawthorne grew even more anxious. Upon their arrival, Ada Shepard left them to sail back to America, after which the Hawthornes found themselves caught in a whirlwind of social engagements, renewing acquaintances with their old friends. Meeting with Fields, Hawthorne learned that his publisher had arranged the sale of his upcoming book to a British publisher. Since the only way he could secure his English copyright was to be in residence on the date of publication, their stay in England stretched into yet another full year.

Finding the coastal village of Redcar to their liking, they settled in and Hawthorne wrote every morning. The isolation of the place was perfect for his work. By November *The Marble Faun* was completed. The book came out in February in England and a few weeks later in America. Now the Hawthornes could go home. After seven years of a nomadic life, the family left England's shores on the *Europa* on June 16 and arrived in America on June 28. They went directly to their home, The Wayside.

During his absence, Hawthorne's letters to Ticknor displayed a wide array of opinions and emotions regarding home. One day he could not wait to come back, the next day he dreaded the return. Hawthorne had also come to realize that he did not care for settling down, but loved to travel and roam about. Now that he looked once again upon his former home, The Wayside lost much of its luster and appeal, especially after living in the grand houses of England and Italy.

Hawthorne's first order of business was to make alterations to The Wayside, one of which was to add a square tower to the top. Here he had hoped to write, but never took into consideration that it would be very hot in summer and very cold in winter. An additional problem was the cost—the final tally came to four times the original estimate. Hawthorne's income was limited and had been hampered by the fact that he had loaned out a large sum to friends, the return of which he would never see. After the addition to the house was complete, he had to admit, it was just plain ugly. Writing to a friend, Hawthorne said it was "the absurdest anomaly you ever saw ..." [Van Doren 235].

The town of Concord no longer held the interest that it had before. Hawthorne turned down many invitations to come and lecture. More and more he kept to himself, spending a great deal of time on the wooded hill behind the house. Slowly but steadily he felt his interest and zest in life ebbing away. The children were growing up and became involved in their own social lives, attending parties, dances, picnics and outings. The girls attended private schools, and Julian was sent to Cambridge in preparation for becoming a Harvard man.

Hawthorne still wrote—mainly because he needed money—
turning out a series of articles for *The Atlantic Monthly*, which later
became the book, *Our Old Home*, published in 1863. Hawthorne turned
once more to his romance based in England. He had started writing the
book in Italy, but he had laid it aside when *The Marble Faun* interfered.
Now he brought it out to make a fresh start.

On April 13, 1861, Sophia wrote in her journal "WAR!!" and
jotted notes about the firing on Fort Sumter by Rebel soldiers. The
onslaught of the Civil War greatly upset Nathaniel Hawthorne and
proved a devastating distraction from his writing. Through the years, his
views of the problems of the country were mixed, but he had never
completely agreed with the abolitionists (of which there were many in
Concord and in his wife's family). Statements made in his letters showed
that Hawthorne thought the North and South to be too diverse to ever
really get along. He was not convinced the Union could be, or should be,
saved. He was, however, completely in sympathy with the North once
war broke out and felt it should be fought to the bitter end.

In March 1862, Hawthorne accepted an invitation from his friend,
Bridge to take a trip to the nation's capital. Ticknor came along to keep
Hawthorne as his companion. The visit lasted a month, during which
Hawthorne saw the war at close range. He visited Fort Monroe,
Manassas, the ironclad *Monitor*, and Harpers Ferry. He saw rotting
carcasses of horses and great stretches of woods destroyed by battles. He
met General McClellan, and even paid a visit to President Lincoln. After
returning home he wrote the article, "Chiefly About War Matters,"
which appeared in the *Atlantic Monthly* in July. His wonderful sketch of
Lincoln was edited out of the final piece, which later was said to be one
of the more realistic and true descriptions of the President.

Following the trip to Washington, D.C., Hawthorne's health grew
worse. There seemed to be no apparent disease, but he was slowly
slipping away. Friends noticed the change in his appearance, the stooped
shoulders and slow walk. Refusing to see a doctor, he pretended nothing
was wrong, but Sophia saw the "exquisite frolic" missing in his eyes and
sensed his restlessness [Van Doren 259]. In an almost desperate state,
Hawthorne returned to his writing, and even permitted Fields to
announce that there would be a forthcoming new work from him. The
existing documents of *The Dolliver Romance* reveal the courage, wit, and
wisdom of the expiring man. After a few weeks, however, Hawthorne

admitted in a letter to Fields that he knew he would never finish the work. That fact did not disturb him so terribly because a part of him was weary and longed for rest. And yet, Hawthorne bravely kept up the front. His daughter Rose remembered that while her father had little appetite during those days, he would still come to the table dressed in his best black coat.

In March 1864, it was decided that Hawthorne should take a trip with Ticknor to New York and Philadelphia. In spite of the cold and rainy weather that followed them, they called on publishers and booksellers in Philadelphia. On the evening of April 8, Ticknor suffered from what Hawthorne called a severe bilious attack. In a freak turn of events, Hawthorne found himself sitting by the bedside of his dying friend until the end, firmly convinced that death had claimed the wrong person. Bravely holding up for the benefit of Ticknor's friends and family, Hawthorne did not break down and weep for his lost friend until his return home. "There are lines ploughed on his brow," Sophia wrote, "which were never there before" [Mellow 576].

In May, knowing how Hawthorne loved the countryside in spring, Pierce suggested the two of them take a carriage trip to Center Harbor. Sophia agreed that it would be a good plan. Once they had started, however, Pierce was surprised to realize just how ill Hawthorne really was. His mind was sluggish, his walking painful, and the use of his hands greatly impaired. Yet, Hawthorne appeared to enjoy seeing the orchards in full bloom. As they rode along Hawthorne conversed with his friend about death: "What a boon it would be, if when life draws to a close, one could pass away without a struggle," he said [Mellow 577].

The two friends stayed that evening, May 12, in the Pemigewasset House in Plymouth, sleeping in adjoining rooms. Pierce decided they would remain there for several days and on the next day he planned to send for Sophia and Una to join them. Around one or two o'clock in the morning Pierce looked in on Hawthorne and realized he had not moved. The great author, and Pierce's life-long friend, was gone.

Rose Hawthorne remembered vividly saying good-bye to her father the morning he left for that last journey. She felt sure he knew he would never return and commented on her father's bravery: "He hated failure, dependence, and disorder, broken rules and weariness of discipline, as he hated cowardice," she wrote. "I cannot express how brave he seemed to me" [Mellow 577].

The funeral took place on May 23 in the Unitarian Church of Concord. Longfellow remembered the town being white with apple blossoms. The Reverend James Freeman Clarke, who twenty-two years before officiated at the wedding of Hawthorne and Sophia, conducted the services. From the church, the procession moved slowly to the Sleepy Hollow Cemetery where, after a few words were spoken, Franklin Pierce sprinkled flowers into the open grave.

After the crowd at the cemetery had dispersed, Sophia Hawthorne's carriage was the last to leave. But as the carriage passed the gate, their son Julian remembered seeing by the gates on either side of the path, Longfellow, Holmes, Lowell, Pierce, Emerson, and half a dozen more. "... As the carriage passed between them, they uncovered their honored heads in honor of Hawthorne's widow." [Hawthorne, J. 348].


## EPILOGUE

Following Hawthorne's death, Sophia dedicated her life to her children, all of whom were very close. She went on to edit some of her husband's journals and published them in a two-volume set entitled, *Passages from the American Notebooks of Nathaniel Hawthorne*. The works came out in 1868, but were followed by a series of rifts with the new publishing house of Fields, Osgood & Company. The problems were so complex that when she published her own reminiscences, *Notes in England and Italy*, she turned to Putnam, a rival firm.

By 1868, Sophia sold The Wayside and moved to Germany. There she and the children settled into an American colony in Dresden. After the outbreak of the Franco-German war, Sophia and the girls moved to London, and Julian returned to America. In the winter of 1870-71, Sophia came down with typhoid pneumonia. She died on February 26, 1871.

Una remained in England and always frail in health, died in 1877, at the young age of thirty-three. She was buried in Kensal Green Cemetery beside her mother.

Julian went on to become a noted author despite the fact that all his works would be forever compared to his father's. He died in 1934, living to the age of eighty-five.

Rose in later years opened a home in New York for indigent persons suffering from incurable diseases like cancer. When she was widowed, she became a nun, Sister Mary Alphonsa, and continued her work with the poor until she died at age seventy-five.

Hawthorne's legacy has not diminished over the years. His works remain classic reading for students today. Movies and television dramas based on his most famous novel, *The Scarlet Letter*, continue to be produced. Called a work of pure genius, *The Scarlet Letter* is a timeless tale that never grows old.

Today, visitors to the town of Salem, Massachusetts can explore the seven-gabled house that inspired Nathaniel Hawthorne to write his novel, *The House of the Seven Gables*. In 1908, Miss Caroline O. Emmerton purchased the house, which was built in 1668, and restored it; in 1910, the house was opened the public.

The Old Manse, where Hawthorne and Sophia began their married life, still stands in Concord and it, too, is an historical landmark open to the public. The Wayside, the only home owned by the Hawthornes, is part of the Minute Man National Historic Park in Concord.

Although Hawthorne was somewhat of an enigma to his contemporaries, he was a much-loved family man, adored by his wife and children. In a letter to Annie Fields, wife of Hawthorne's friend and publisher, James Fields, Sophia extolled her late husband's virtues: "A person of a more uniform majesty never wore mortal form. In the most retired privacy, it was the same as in the presence of men.... A tenderness so infinite—so embracing—that God's alone could surpass it. It folded the loathsome leper in as soft a caress as the child of his home affections—was not that divine!" [Mellow 578].

## WORKS CITED

Gaeddert, Louann. *A New England Love Story*. New York: Dial Press, 1980.

Hawthorne, Hildegarde. *Romantic Rebel*. New York: Hawthorne Books, Inc., 1932.

Hawthorne, Julian. *Hawthorne and His Wife, A Biography in Two Volumes*. New York: Houghton, Mifflin & Co., 1884.

Mellow, James R. *Nathaniel Hawthorne In His Times.* Boston: Houghton
    Mifflin Co., 1980.
Turner, Arlin. *Nathaniel Hawthorne, A Biography.* Oxford: Oxford
    University Press, 1980.
Van Doren, Mark. *Nathaniel Hawthorne, A Critical Biography.* New York:
    The Viking Press, 1949.

NEIL HEIMS

# An Introduction to Some Elements
# of Nathaniel Hawthorne's Fiction

## I. EMBLEMS

Wherever you look in the fiction of Nathaniel Hawthorne, you see emblems: a scarlet letter A, a seven gabled house, a blood stain, a purple flower expelling a poisonous breath, a black veil, a set of pink ribbons, a serpentine walking stick, a Maypole, a lime kiln, a hidden tree house, Praxiteles' marble representation of a faun, a Lady's mantle, a snow image, a birthmark, a tower, a bosom serpent. The proliferation of emblems in Hawthorne's writing alerts us that they are allegories and that the stories go beyond the regional, historic, pastoral and gothic boundaries which generate and define them. Sometimes, Hawthorne himself tells us, as in the opening paragraph of "The Threefold Destiny," when he writes that the story he is about to tell, "[r]ather than claiming to be real ... may be considered as an allegory." (*Twice Told Tales*, 322) While, of course, real or unreal, the stories Hawthorne writes are about what they say they are about, they are also, as Angus Fletcher observed, as allegories, about something else:

> "The Birthmark" leaves the reader with a gradually more
> sure sense that the birthmark is the insignia of life itself, by
> virtue of the imperfection it implies, and such in fact turns

49

out to be the case when Aylmer finally succeeds in removing the birthmark from his wife's body. In "Rappaccini's Daughter" Hawthorne moves in two directions at once; while the action becomes increasingly restless and dramatic, the iconography settles into an increasingly sure interpretive pattern, so that at the close of the story we have a fixed idea of the particular contagion that is attached to Rappaccini's garden. (Fletcher, 82-83)

Emblems suggest things other than what they manifestly represent and therefore, alert us to seek embedded meaning. Leo Marx argued of *The Scarlet Letter*, for example, that as an allegorical romance it is "a highly stylized symbolic fable, and only in its moral significance is it firmly linked with the world we inhabit." (Marx, xi) Even if this judgment is overstated, allegorical works do generate such questions as: What is this really about? What are the emblems telling us?

One of Hawthorne's most revealing emblems is the Pilgrims' ship, *The Mayflower*. Using this legendary vessel as an emblem, Hawthorne represents the underlying concern of his work: understanding the elements that comprise and define the human condition. The emblem appears toward the end of an essay written in July 1862, during the Civil War, for *The Atlantic Monthly* magazine, "Chiefly about War Matters." The essay is an account of his journey to Washington D.C. and parts of Virginia from his home in Massachusetts "while it was still the long, dreary January of our Northern year, though March in name." It is perhaps one of the oddest pieces of American political journalism and war reportage ever, being rather a meditation on solitude, fancy, and history with a series of depictions of landscapes, towns and personages, including President Abraham Lincoln, in a manner recognizably Hawthorne's. It is also, ironically, tempered with Hawthorne's interpolated footnotes, which often take issue with the text.

Coming across some escaping slaves in Virginia as he toured a Union army post there, Hawthorne presents them as "a party of contrabands, escaping out of the mysterious depths of Secessia" and proceeds as if they were allegorical figures in one of his romances:

They were unlike the specimens of their race whom we are accustomed to see at the North, and, in my judgment, were far more agreeable. So rudely were they attired,—as if their garb had grown upon them spontaneously,—so picturesquely natural in manners, and wearing such a crust of primeval simplicity (which is quite polished away from the northern black man), that they seemed a kind of creature by themselves, not altogether human, but perhaps quite as good, and akin to the fauns and rustic deities of olden times.

From the pens of many other writers, this passage might well appear reprehensible and condescending, but it is not from Hawthorne's. In this passage he endows the fugitive slaves with the same quality he attributes to Donatello in the opening chapters of *The Marble Faun*, before that carefree Italian count hurls his own innocence from the Tarpeian Rock in Rome as he flings from it the man who is tormenting his beloved Miriam. Donatello in those early sections and the fugitive slaves in the magazine piece represent an ideal of spontaneity and innocence for Hawthorne. They are emblems for and examples of pre-lapsarian consciousness and its harmonious connection to the operations of Nature. But the innocence they represent, just because human passion, will, and desire exist as part of our nature, is an innocence which Hawthorne sees as therefore under threat from passion, will, and desire. But innocence also signifies an undeveloped humanity. He shares a Miltonic sense of the Fall as being necessary to mankind—as he shows by the growth of Donatello's character—for the development of both consciousness and the capacity for virtuous choice.

The Fall, as Hawthorne sees it, is endlessly recapitulated in human action. Virtuous intelligence is available to us, in Hawthorne's view, only after we have committed ourselves sinfully and have had to grapple with the ensuing guilt. Then, as is the case with Donatello, we can become capable of consciousness and virtue rather than only the natural spontaneity of mere being. Paradoxically, the fall from an original grace, as with Donatello and Arthur Dimmesdale, too, in *The Scarlet Letter*, is the instrument which brings its victim to a "higher," albeit painful, realization of what it is to be human. It turns the doctrine of the *felix culpa*, the fortunate fall of Christianity whereby Adam's fault enables Christ's victory, into an emblem for a defining human psychological process. We realize ourselves by overcoming our transgressions. Discovering how to overcome them, as is the case with many of

Hawthorne's characters, is the way we learn who we are. In Hawthorne's tales this is not necessarily a happy knowledge.

Thus, Hawthorne sees human experience, like Judeo-Christian history itself, as divided into two contiguous and opposite modes: the Golden Age of paradise and the present burden of the fallen world—innocence and guilt. He appears to think, furthermore, that because of the recurring opportunities to sin or to refrain from sinning, Original Sin is not *inherent in* our nature but an *inherent capability of* our nature, which we therefore have recurring opportunities to defeat. In "Fancy's Show Box," one of his *Twice Told Tales*, Hawthorne writes:

> In truth there is no such thing in man's nature as a settled and full resolve, either for good or evil, except at the very moment of execution. Let us hope, therefore, that all the dreadful consequences of sin will not be incurred, unless the act have set its seal upon the thought. (138)

Since sinning is the act of transgressing the boundaries proper to humanity and the result of an inexperienced human nature, the fundamental subject of Hawthorne's work—exploring the proper limits of humanity and discovering the uses of sin—provides his readers with an immunizing experience. The capacity to choose virtue and to act virtuously can in part be effected through literature. This justification is important to Hawthorne. In "The Custom-House," the prefatory sketch introducing *The Scarlet Letter*, he imagines a conversation between his Puritan ancestors indicating the contempt with which, he believes, they must view his trade:

> "What is he?" "A writer of story-books! What kind of business in life,—what mode of glorifying God, or being serviceable to mankind in his day and generation,—may that be? Why, the degenerate fellow might as well have been a fiddler!" (*The Scarlet Letter*, 10).

Not surprisingly, then, given his lineage and its history, in Hawthorne's view, there is an inherently dark and destructive side to human nature. After all, these same condemnatory ancestors were the persecutors of Quakers, "witches," and "Indians." They were also, as the ones who expropriated and built upon their property, the shadows behind Colonel Pyncheon in *The House of the Seven Gables*. The war he is writing of in "Chiefly about War Matters" also provides him with evidence that our fundamental nature is amoral. Reporting his impressions of the hale disposition of a Union soldier in Virginia, Hawthorne writes of

> the exhilarating sense of danger,—to kill men blamelessly, or to be killed gloriously,—and to be happy in following out [the] native instincts of destruction.

In "The Artist of the Beautiful," a fantastically wrought mechanical butterfly represents the beauty of an unfettered spirit. Near congenial folk, it flourishes. Near those who scorn freedom of spirit, it wilts. Using this indicator, and using a child as his instrument, Hawthorne subverts the doctrine that goodness and innocence are one and the same:

> As if the butterfly, like the artist, were conscious of something not entirely congenial in the child's nature, it alternately sparkled and grew dim. At length it arose from the small hand of the infant with an airy motion that seemed to bear it upward without an effort..... Had there been no obstruction, it might have soared into the sky and grown immortal. But its lustre gleamed upon the ceiling; the exquisite texture of its wings brushed against that earthly medium; and a sparkle or two, as of stardust, floated downward and lay glimmering on the carpet. Then the butterfly came fluttering down, and, instead of returning to the infant, was apparently attracted towards the artist's hand.
>
> "Not so! not so!" murmured Owen Warland, as if his handiwork could have understood him. "Thou has gone forth out of thy master's heart. There is no return for thee."
>
> With a wavering movement, and emitting a tremulous radiance, the butterfly struggled, as it were, towards the infant, and was about to alight upon his finger; but while it still hovered in the air, the little child of strength, with his

grandsire's sharp and shrewd expression in his face, made a
snatch at the marvellous insect and compressed it in his hand.

Beauty in itself, for Hawthorne, is not transgressive as it largely
was for his ancestors; it is, rather, one of the vehicles by means of which
the artist conveys his inquiry. Hawthorne's Puritan heritage, moreover,
makes him familiar with an aspect of human nature which is rigid,
controlling, averse to the delights of beauty and fancy. Its rationale was
to prevent mankind from surrendering to passion or appetite and to
avoid sin and its consequences. This is just the recipe, Hawthorne's tales
postulate, which sabotages human virtue. Hawthorne's fiction
recognizes, describes and endeavors to deconstruct this Puritanical
sternness. Reading Hawthorne can help lessen our disposition to
succumb to a narrow understanding of what being human means—this
is one of the consequences of the complex structure of so many of his
tales—and because of that very narrowness to fall into sin. He confronts
sin through literature rather than law, eschewing the bitter methods,
medicines, and paradoxical consequences of Puritanism, which in its
constrictive grasp on human being gives added power to sin.

The many ways we can fall from innocence, and the consequences
and conflicts which follow seem to be the sparks for Hawthorne's creative
imagination. As Henry James observed, by transforming Puritan doctrine
into aesthetic material, Hawthorne's stories contemplate moral conflicts
and revolve around moral problems and moral choices—or being blind to
them. (James, 57-58) Epitomizing Hawthorne, James concluded:

> He combined in a singular degree the spontaneity of the
> imagination with a haunting care for moral problems. Man's
> conscience was his theme, but he saw it in the light of a
> creative fancy.... (177)

Hawthorne's art, James suggests, explores the interplay of and,
often, the conflict between problems relating to desire ("the spontaneity
of the imagination") and action ("moral problems") and the shifting
boundaries where the infinite (desire) and the finite (action) meet and
exert pressure upon each other. Additionally, Hawthorne's tales are
critiques of the nature and efficacy of conflicting values with which
moral problems can be met.

In the case of his description of the fleeing slaves, Hawthorne realizes that his allegorization may appear to be a form of dehumanization, and addresses the anticipated rebuke:

> I wonder whether I shall excite anybody's wrath by saying this. It is no great matter. At all events, I felt most kindly towards these poor fugitives, but knew not precisely what to wish in their behalf, nor in the least how to help them. For the sake of the manhood which is latent in them, I would not have turned them back.

He is not saying, even as he uses them emblematically that these persons lack humanity even under present circumstances or are inherently devoid of manhood. They are unpracticed in it because enslavement is a counter condition to manhood, denying the ability to exercise responsibility. It keeps the enslaved in a state of debased innocence. He then uses the two conditions of mankind as emblematized by the oppressed and innocent blacks and the oppressing and guilty whites to construct a more encompassing emblem. Within this emblem—*The Mayflower*—the metaphors of black and white are contained, and the polarities which determine Hawthorne's vision of mankind as well as of human action are established:

> There is an historical circumstance, known to few, that connects the children of the Puritans with these Africans of Virginia in a very singular way. They are our brethren, as being lineal descendants from the Mayflower, the fated womb of which, in her first voyage, sent forth a brood of Pilgrims on Plymouth Rock, and, in a subsequent one, spawned slaves upon the Southern soil,—a monstrous birth, but with which we have an instinctive sense of kindred, and so are stirred by an irresistible impulse to attempt their rescue, even at the cost of blood and ruin. The character of our sacred ship, I fear, may suffer a little by this revelation; but we must let her white progeny offset her dark one,—and two such portents never sprang from an identical source before.

The words "white" "dark" and "progeny" no longer refer only to the two races but to the nature and consequences of the two cargoes—

pilgrims and slaves—and consequently to the two aspects of the human condition. *The Mayflower* becomes the original bearer of people to tyranny and debasement as well as to liberty and possibility. It is made to represent the womb of innocence and of guilt. Inside the vision that generates Hawthorne's fiction *The Mayflower* becomes emblematic of the inextricable union of good and evil as they are depicted in John Milton's *Areopagitica* as springing from one womb and cleaving to each other, being each the means by which the other is known.

## II. ANTINOMIES

The value conflicts, which pervade and, in fact, govern Hawthorne's fiction, appear in the foreground in his early story, "The Maypole of Merry Mount." Beginning as what appears to be a mirthful sketch of youthful merry-making, it concludes as a Puritanical caution against the distractions of earth-bound delight. As such, Hawthorne announces in a prefatory note to the story,

> the facts recorded on the grave pages of our New England annalists [from which he drew for the story], have wrought themselves, almost spontaneously, into a sort of allegory. (TTT, 35)

As is evident from the closing sentences of the story, it is the allegory of the expulsion from Eden:

> Endicott, the severest Puritan of all ... lifted the wreath of roses from the ruin of the Maypole, and threw it ... over the heads of the Lord and Lady of the May. It was a deed of prophecy. As the moral gloom of the world overpowers all ... gaiety, even so was their home of wild mirth made desolate.... They returned to it no more.... They went heavenward, supporting each other along the difficult path which it was their lot to tread, and never wasted one regretful thought on the vanities of Merry Mount. (47)

The shift from mirth to discipline that the tale narrates constitutes the drama of the story, which is otherwise a rendition of colonial customs, conflicts and commentary upon them. "Bright were the days at Merry Mount," Hawthorne begins

> when the Maypole was the banner staff of that gay colony! They who reared it, should their banner be triumphant, were to pour sunshine on New England's rugged hills, and scatter flower seeds throughout the soil. (35)

But "[j]ollity and gloom were contending for an empire." Hawthorne continues: Set against the colony of mirth at Merry Mount,

> [u]nfortunately, there were men in the new world of a sterner faith than these Maypole worshippers.... a settlement of Puritans, most dismal wretches, who said their prayers before daylight, and then wrought in the forest or the cornfield, till evening made it prayer time again. Their weapons were always at hand, to shoot down the straggling savage. When they met in conclave, it was never to keep up the old English mirth, but to hear sermons three hours long.... Their festivals were fast days, and their chief pastime the singing of psalms. Woe to the youth or maiden who did but dream of a dance! The selectmen nodded to the constable; and there sat the light-heeled reprobate in the stocks; or if he danced, it was round the whipping post, which might be termed the Puritan Maypole. (42)

Here are the two poles—the Maypole and the Whipping Post— that establish the boundaries of Hawthorne's fiction and define the character of the opponents whose conflicts provide its subjects:

> ... a feud arose, stern and bitter on the one side, and as serious on the other as anything could be among such light spirits as had sworn allegiance to the Maypole. The future complexion of New England was involved in this important quarrel. Should the grisly saints establish their jurisdiction over the gay sinners, then would their spirits darken all the clime, and make it a land of clouded visages, of hard toil, of

sermon and psalm forever. But should the banner staff of
Merry Mount be fortunate, sunshine would break upon the
hills, and flowers would beautify the forest.... (43)

"Grisly saints and ... gay sinners" is a peculiar way of classifying.
Gloom is the medium of the saints; sunshine, flowers and beauty, of the
sinners. Accordingly—it seems Hawthorne is writing from, even if not
advocating the Puritanical view—it is good to undergo hardship, bad to
have a free and lightsome enjoyment of life. This is either bitter paradox
or rebellious irony. If paradox, then Hawthorne's is a stern and tragic
vision; if irony, an angry, skeptical, critical one; if both simultaneously,
the beginning of wisdom, indicating a doctrine of ambiguity. This
ambiguity continues to the end of the tale. The narrator's lesson that the
defeated denizens of Merry Mount "never wasted one regretful thought
on the vanities of Merry Mount" indicates both an endorsement of the
change and an ironic repudiation of it. The tale itself shows the
narrator's delight in mirth, and many readers may experience at least a
twinge of regret at the loss, unless, of course, Puritan influence has so
hardened them to mirth. This bipolar conflict, emblematized by the
Maypole and the whipping post, not only sets groups or individuals
against each other, but also puts individuals at odds with themselves. It
is the shaping contradiction of Hawthorne's art and forms the basis for
most of his plots, and it is at the root of the anguish of many of his
characters.

    After the triumph of Puritanism, the struggle is not only the
struggle between mirth and gloom, nature and religion, authority and
spontaneity, or disobedience and obedience, but between hiding or
revealing transgressions against Puritanical strictures. This struggle
provides an anatomy of guiltiness. In *The Scarlet Letter*, Hawthorne
establishes the context for the struggle and its anatomy by the forbidden
act of sexual intercourse between the minister, Arthur Dimmesdale and
Hester Prynne. Pregnancy brings the transgression to the foreground,
but only regarding the woman, not the minister. In her refusal to identify
her partner, Hester protects him from public humiliation but exposes
him to the pains of his own awareness and a sense of gnawing guilt. She
leaves him to his own strength—or weakness—by not denouncing him,
and leaves him the burden of making or failing to make his own
confession.

The society that determined the austere character of Arthur Dimmesdale (and the lure of his transgression) is characterized in the book's first sentence, emblematically, as:

> [a] throng of bearded men, in sad-colored garments and gray, steeple-crowned hats, intermixed with women, some wearing hoods, and others bareheaded ... assembled in front of a wooden edifice, the door of which was heavily timbered with oak, and studded with iron spikes. (49)

Three paragraphs later in the second chapter, Hawthorne amplifies his picture of this folk:

> Amongst any other population, or at a later period of the history of New England, the grim rigidity that petrified the bearded physiognomies of these good people would have augured some awful business in hand. It could have betokened nothing short of the anticipated execution of some noted culprit.... But, in that early severity of the Puritan character, an inference of this kind could not so indubitably be drawn. It might be that a sluggish bond-servant, or an undutiful child, whom his parents had given over to the civil authority, was to be corrected at the whipping-post. It might be that an antinomian Quaker, or other heterodox religionist, was to be scourged out of town, or an idle and vagrant Indian, whom the white man's fire-water had made riotous about the streets, was to be driven with stripes into the shadow of the forest.... In either case, there was very much the same solemnity of demeanour on the part of the spectators; as befitted a people amongst whom religion and law were almost identical, and in whose character both were so thoroughly interfused, that the mildest and the severest acts of public discipline were alike made venerable and awful. Meager, indeed, and cold was the sympathy that a transgressor might look for, from such bystanders at the scaffold. (51-52)

The spectators, it is easy to see, are of the party of the whipping post, not the Maypole. Their grim severity is the rule. Their wrath against Hester is fierce as a result of her venture to the party of the Maypole. One of the gossips gathered around the prison door waiting to view Hester Prynne's public shaming cries:

> "The magistrates are God-fearing gentlemen, but merciful overmuch.... At the very least, they should have put the brand of a hot iron on Hester Prynne's forehead." (53)

Between the portrayal of the crowd in front of the prison and the one assembled in the market place, Hawthorne lights on "[a] wild rose bush covered, in this month of June, with its delicate gems" beside the prison door. "Finding it," Hawthorne concludes the first chapter,

> so directly on the threshold of our narrative, which is now about to issue from that inauspicious portal, we could hardly do otherwise than pluck one of its flowers and present it to the reader. It may serve, let us hope, to symbolize some sweet moral blossom, that may be found along the track, or relieve the darkening close of a tale of human frailty and sorrow. (50)

Rather than mistaking this passage for a flowery mordent indicating the sentimental practice of a nineteenth-century author, not advancing plot, philosophy, or characterization, let us recognize it as a vital element in the chromatics of the story. In a novel which depicts people for whom dun is the hue of morality, here is a rose presented by the author's own hand as a "sweet moral blossom." It is as if Hawthorne were telegraphing the reader from beyond his tale that colorlessness is not the only fitting human possibility, that sweetness can be moral, and morality sweet, not always of the sour variety of Puritanism. Hawthorne, moreover, defines his tale as one "of human frailty and sorrow," not of sin and disobedience, as for example Milton does in *Paradise Lost*, where, in his account of the Fall, humanity is characterized not as frail but as "sufficient to stand." Hawthorne's narrator does not present the trespasses recounted in *The Scarlet Letter* primarily as offenses against the Divinity, but against humanity, against others and against oneself. His story is not about our relation to God, but to ourselves and to each other. Because of the multiplicity of perspectives built into the narrative through conflicting elements—what Hawthorne called showing "different sides of the same dark idea to the reader's eye," (*Letters, 1843-1853*, 307)—it is difficult to limit the transgression to one action only or to the deed of but one character. The frailty of which Hawthorne tells is of several sorts.

Certainly, the wrong which *The Scarlet Letter* explores can be the act of forbidden sexual intercourse between Hester Prynne and Dimmesdale. It violates social regulation and religious stricture, yet when Hawthorne speaks of that offense, while viewing it as a transgression against a "sacred law," he mitigates it, "... this had been a sin of passion, not of principle, nor even purpose." (208) Hawthorne is speaking here with regard to the minister, not Hester. The novel is an anatomy of Minister Dimmesdale's failure. He stands neither by his deepest religious beliefs, nor by the rules of his community, nor by the call of his nature, nor by his partner in the act who suffers social disgrace and gathers no comfort from him. Yet, he is not painted as a villain. He is shown as a deeply suffering man, striving to do good, weak and in need of human comfort. He is aware of a wretchedness of person which pains but does not shock him. It accords with the very picture of human nature that the Puritanism of the whipping post has trained him to believe is authentic.

Hester Prynne herself is a characteristic type in eighteenth- and nineteenth-century novels, the fallen woman. When Hawthorne's narrator first speaks of the offense of unconsecrated and ecclesiastically unlegitimated sexual intercourse with regard to her, he refers to it as

> the taint of deepest sin in the most sacred quality of human
> life, working such effect, that the world was only the darker
> for this woman's beauty, and the more lost for the infant that
> she had borne. (58)

But neither Hester nor the infant, Pearl, despite this severe language—a reading of verses three to eleven in the eighth chapter of *The Gospel According to St. John* regarding the woman taken in adultery might indicate *overly* severe language,—neither Hester nor Pearl is presented throughout *The Scarlet Letter* this way. Hawthorne does not show the world as darkened by Hester, even though he shows darkness clinging to her, nor lost because of Pearl, who often appears as the very emblem of life. Despite how much the novel emphasizes the amount of shame her community attaches to her and the degree to which her mortification affects the course of her days, Hester is depicted neither as worthy of the reader's scorn nor pity. She is shown neither as a victim nor *in herself*, omitting the passionate slip of nature, as a morally culpable or debased person. Her generosity of spirit, lack of bitterness and performance of helpful and charitable works are shown throughout the novel:

> Hester sought not to acquire any thing beyond a subsistence, of the plainest and most ascetic description, for herself, and a simple abundance for her child.... Hester  bestowed all her superfluous means in charity, on wretches less miserable than herself, and who not unfrequently insulted the hand that fed them. (86)

She accepts her punishment and remains in Boston bearing her badge of shame when she might have gone from the colony to lead a life unmarked by her offense. Hawthorne allows her two reasons. The first, because it rises from desires born of human passion, he characterizes, according to the values and beliefs of the society in which he is locating his narrative, as an idea diabolically inspired. Indeed Hawthorne echoes the kind of longing Dante describes in his depiction of the eternal punishment of Paolo and Francesca in the fifth canto of *Inferno*:

> There dwelt, there trod the feet of one with whom she deemed herself connected in a union, that, unrecognized on earth, would bring them together before the bar of final judgment, and make their marriage-altar, for a joint futurity of endless retribution. (83)

But it is not a fantasy Hester herself fully approves; she is torn between her human being and the religious imperatives and definitions of her community:

> She barely looked the idea in the face, and hastened to bar it in its dungeon. What she compelled herself to believe,— what, finally, she reasoned upon, as her motive for continuing a resident of New England,—was half a truth,

and half a self-delusion. Here, she said to herself, had been the scene of her guilt, and here should be the scene of her earthly punishment; and so, perchance, the torture of her daily shame would at length purge her soul, and work out another purity than that which she had lost; more saint-like, because the result of martyrdom. (83-84)

Even the Puritan ritual of displaying her on the marketplace scaffold—"a portion of the penal machine," Hawthorne calls it—holding her baby, to bear the contumely of her righteous neighbors, is described in terms which mix grace and disgrace in the reader's imagination. The tableau is given dialectical readings:

Had there been a Papist among the crowd of Puritans, he might have seen in this beautiful woman, so picturesque in attire and mien, and with the infant at her bosom, an object to remind him of the image of Divine Maternity, which so many illustrious painters have vied with one another to represent. (58)

After Hawthorne plants this image, he erases it, asserting the morality of the society he is limning, and uses the image to show what Hester is not. The first impression, however, the image of Hester as Mary, is as strong as its repudiation, which occurs mid-sentence when Hawthorne explains that the image of Hester as the Madonna ought to be

something which should remind him [the Catholic who chanced to be among the crowd], indeed, but only by contrast, of that sacred image of sinless motherhood, whose infant was to redeem the world.

Tangentially, his first view of Hester also suggests, in a world dedicated to an unbending vision of moral absolutes, that what appears to be and what is can, in fact, differ. It is not at all clear, also, that Pearl does not in some important way "redeem the world," within the context of *The Scarlet Letter,* from the life-defying, life-denying severity of the harsh Puritans who cannot comprehend her.

The "human frailty" referred to in the closing sentence of the first chapter, whose consequence is grief and sorrow, may be the very gloom and sternness of Puritanism itself, which deny the vivacity or complexity of life, and provoke violation through excessive constraint. Hawthorne sets these several elements against each other, examines them all with objectivity, as Henry James asserts (57, 110) and discredits any single-minded vision of rectitude. Even the specific image of the Madonna serves not only to suggest and deny for Hester herself the stature of martyrdom. It also infuses into the monochrome mono-dimensionality of Puritanism a contrasting sacred understanding of human faith. Anathema though the Catholic vision is to the Puritans of whom he writes, it is not entirely so to Hawthorne himself. In *The Marble Faun*, for example, he endows the good, Puritanical New England maiden, Hilda, with reverence for the Virgin and respect for several other Catholic symbols, mysteries and practices.

Perhaps the most serious challenge to the Puritan ethos which determines the action and psychology of *The Scarlet Letter* is the alternative embodied in the figure of Hester's child, Pearl. She is represented as possessing "never-failing vivacity of spirits," and as not having "the disease of sadness." Hawthorne calls her, "that little creature, whose innocent life had sprung, by the inscrutable decree of Providence, a lovely and immortal flower."(92) She is not, with regard to the Divinity, illegitimate. Likened to a flower, she is emblematically joined to that first flower from the rosebush beside the prison door, which Hawthorne offered the reader at the outset in mitigation of the ensuing gloom of his tale. In fact, Pearl is painted as a redeemer:

> God, as a direct consequence of the sin which man thus punished [by marking it with the scarlet letter on Hester's bosom], had given her a lovely child, whose place was on that same dishonored bosom, to connect her parent for ever with the race and descent of mortals, and to be finally a blessed soul in heaven! (92)

This is contrary to both the earlier narrative pronouncement that "the world was ... the more lost" because of her birth and the inverse comparison of her to Mary's child, "the infant [who] was to redeem the world." (58) Pearl embodies a disposition contrary to the Puritan ideal.

She is suffused with radiance. Hawthorne calls her "worthy to have been brought forth in Eden; worthy to have been left there, to be the play thing of the angels." (93) (Her innocence, although untempered by a redeeming Hawthornian guilt is nevertheless depicted here as sacred, perhaps because it has sprung from and is in some sense a resolution of that guilt.) Changeable in aspect, Hawthorne writes of her, she

> was imbued with a spell of infinite variety; in this one child there were many children, comprehending the full scope between the wild-flower prettiness of a peasant-baby, and the pomp, in little, of an infant princess. Throughout all [he concludes], however, there was a trait of passion, a certain depth of hue, which she never lost. (93)

It is a warm and sympathetic description of the child. Hawthorne continues: "Her nature appeared to possess depth, too, as well as variety." But:

> The child could not be made amenable to rules. In giving her existence, a great law had been broken; and the result was a being, whose elements were perhaps beautiful and brilliant, but all in disorder; or with an order peculiar to themselves, amidst which the point of variety and arrangement was difficult or impossible to be discovered. (94)

Even here, the narrator does not devalue Pearl. We'd expect him to say about her, as he first does—given the Puritan moral context of the story—that her attributes were "in disorder." But he revises himself immediately and says, remarkably for his context—subverting it—"or with an order peculiar to themselves." This defies the Puritan insistence that theirs is the only order and anything else is disorder. Pearl represents the mystery and the variety of life. Puritanism denies both through its doctrinal certainty and its consequent rigidity. Through Pearl, too, Hawthorne legitimates individuality and challenges the binding of individuals to a single absolute identity.

Hawthorne continues to use Pearl as a foil for the Puritan character as he describes her encounters with other children:

She saw the children of the settlement, on the grassy margin of the street, or at the domestic thresholds, disporting themselves in such grim fashion as the Puritan nature would permit; playing at going to church, perchance; or at scourging Quakers.... Pearl saw, and gazed intently, but never sought to make acquaintance. If spoken to, she would not speak again. If the children gathered about her, as they sometimes did, Pearl would grow positively terrible in her puny wrath, snatching up stones to fling at them. (97)

A phenomenological description like this one, however, does not show motives and Hawthorne proceeds to explains Pearl's wrath not as a devilish accretion corrupting her, but as a response to an accurate reading of the others' characters and behavior:

The truth was, that the little Puritans, being of the most intolerant brood that ever lived, had got a vague idea of something outlandish, unearthly, or at variance with ordinary fashions, in mother and child; and therefore scorned them in their hearts, and not infrequently reviled them with their tongues. Pearl felt the sentiment, and requited it with the bitterest hatred that can be supposed to rankle in a childish bosom. (97)

Pearl is of the party of the Maypole, mirthful and moody, connected to nature and people, aware of what is underneath what appears to be, as her insight into the characters and the mystery of her parents shows. The Puritan condemnation of her rests on the argument that this wildness undoes morality. It does, for Pearl does not function by rules, yet through her Hawthorne shows how there is a beneficial regulation in nature that simply happens:

Perceiving a flock of beach-birds, that fed and fluttered along the shore, the naughty child picked up her apron full of pebbles, and, creeping from rock to rock after these small sea-fowl, displayed remarkable dexterity in pelting them. One little gray bird, with a white breast, Pearl was almost sure, had been hit by a pebble, and fluttered away with a broken wing. But the elf-child sighed, and gave up her sport; because it grieved her to have done harm to a little being that was as wild as the sea-breeze or as wild as Pearl herself. (183–184)

There is natural affinity between beings when they can penetrate each other's sensibilities, which the imposition of authority prevents. The Puritans are thus virtuous (when they are) by constraint rather than by nature. Consequently by the force set in motion by constraint, they spawn that black world which they then believe requires their strictures to combat, as Hawthorne shows in "Young Goodman Brown" when he devises a character who enters the mirror world that Puritanism projects. The fear of intimacy with his wife causes Goodman Brown to remove himself from her, then to imagine his desire for her as evil. This vision causes him then to establish in his mind the suspicion that evil and violation rather than goodness and accord rule people's hearts and their passions.

Pearl pelts the bird, but then a natural morality based on consciousness comes into play. Hawthorne, in fact, constructs the sentence in such a way that Pearl becomes the subject of the sentence, not the bird which had seemed to be, thus establishing Pearl as the active center of consciousness: "One little ... bird, ... Pearl was almost sure, had been hit." She is not removed from her own experience or from the experience of the other. As the delayed subject in the penultimate sentence and as the content of the concluding sentence indicate, Pearl identifies herself with them. This is natural morality and intuitive knowledge. It stands in contrast both to Puritan morality and to the learning which applies itself for ill—alienated from sympathy with another—in order to quench the appetite of its practitioner.

Such is the case for Roger Chillingworth, whose fall *The Scarlet Letter* also explores. His role is tormentor. Insinuating himself as his physician, for both body and mind, into the confidence of Arthur Dimmesdale, who is ailing of guilt and wasting away, he increases Dimmesdale's agony, rather than relieving him. A diabolical figure, Hawthorne describes him as throwing "a dark light on Hester's state of mind." (183) His fault is one which is repeatedly presented in Hawthorne's fiction, perhaps most notably in "Ethan Brand." It is the stony-heartedness of "cold and remorseless purpose" which can make another "the subject of a psychological experiment," and thereby waste, absorb and perhaps annihilate the other's soul. (*Celestial Railroad and Other Stories*, 280) Dimmesdale characterizes Chillingworth accurately when he tells Hester, "He has violated, in cold blood, the sanctity of a human heart. Thou and I Hester, never did." (202) Hawthorne describes Chillingworth as one of those "skillful men" who are, because of the very power of their skill, insufficient:

> In their researches into the human frame, it may be that the higher and more subtle faculties of such men were materialized, and they lost the spiritual view of existence amid the intricacies of that wondrous mechanism, which seemed to involve art enough to comprise all of life within itself. (122)

He is not characterized, however, as insufficient in the ability to see into a person's heart. He gains entrance into Dimmesdale's bosom. He is practiced in medicinal and psychological arts. Hawthorne describes his strategy. "In Arthur Dimmesdale," he writes,

> thought and imagination were so active, and sensibility so intense, that the bodily infirmity would be likely to have its groundwork there. So Roger Chillingworth ... strove to go deep into his patient's bosom, delving among his principles, prying into his recollections, and probing everything with a cautious touch, like a treasure-seeker in a dark cavern. (127)

Describing his method, Hawthorne writes a succinct monograph on psychotherapy, theory and practice:

> Few secrets can escape an investigator, who has opportunity and license to undertake such a quest, and skill to follow it up.... If [he] possess native sagacity, and a nameless something more,—let us call it intuition; if he show no intrusive egoism, nor disagreeably prominent characteristics of his own; if he have the power ... to bring his mind into such affinity with his patient's, that this last shall unawares have spoken what he imagines himself only to have thought;

if such revelations be received without tumult, and acknowledged not so often by an uttered sympathy, as by silence, an inarticulate breath, and here and there a word, to indicate that all is understood; if, to these qualifications of a confidant be joined the advantages afforded by his recognized character as a physician;—then, at some inevitable moment, will the soul of the sufferer be dissolved, and flow forth in a dark, but transparent stream, bringing all its mysteries into the daylight. (127–128)

Chillingworth's learning is a source of power, not of wisdom. His fault is dual. His violation of the sanctity of another's bosom, is matched by the collateral fault of using knowledge not to enhance, sanctify or glorify it, but to violate life. His power exists, moreover, only because Dimmesdale needs to hide. When Dimmesdale acknowledges his partnership with Hester, Chillingworth's power withers.

## III. Kinds of Power

After Clifford and Hepzibah Pyncheon discover their wicked and duplicitous cousin Jaffrey Pyncheon, a corrupt judge and an ambitious politician, dead in a chair beneath the portrait of their mutual ancestor, whose picture and whose original story of expropriation and murder haunt *The House of the Seven Gables*, they embark on a fantastic railroad journey. Clifford, after a life defined by aestheticism and sensuality and by thirty years of wrongful imprisonment—as a victim of Judge Pyncheon—after years of mental torpor and indecisiveness, offers an energetic soliloquy to his fellow passengers in praise of the forces of progress:

"Then there is electricity—the demon, the angel, the mighty physical power, the all-pervading intelligence!" exclaimed Clifford. "Is that a humbug, too? Is it a fact—or have I dreamt it—that, by means of electricity, the world of matter has become a great nerve, vibrating thousands of miles in a breathless world of time? Rather, the round globe is a vast head, a brain, instinct with intelligence! Or, shall we say, it is itself a thought, nothing but thought, and no longer the substance which we deem it!" (House of Seven Gables, 230)

During Hawthorne's lifetime traditional ideas of nature and reality and the sense of what is within the command of human power were being challenged. Scientific accomplishment—Clifford's example is electricity—often made speculation begin to appear like actual possibility. Mesmerism and the discovery of anesthesia cast the old ideas of demonic possession into new forms. Distinctions between belief, magic and science could not be clearly delineated, nor could the boundaries between the material and the spiritual world. The belief that there is an invisible as well as a visible reality, that the boundary between actual and imaginary possibilities is indefinite, that there are metaphysical explanations for physical events and supernatural causes of natural phenomena, certainly, had always existed. Religious belief has always postulated a realm of invisible and supernatural power. Puritanism authorized, as all religions, probably by their very nature, traditionally do, a belief in the power of an invisible world. Here is Cotton Mather concluding an accusation of witchcraft against Rebecca Nurse on the subject in *Memorable Providences*:

> I am resolv'd after this, never to use but just one grain of patience with any man that shall go to impose upon me a Denial of Devils, or of Witches. I shall count that man Ignorant who shall suspect, but I shall count him down-right Impudent if he Assert the Non-Existence of things which we have had such palpable. Convictions of. I am sure he cannot be a Civil, (and some will question whether he can be an honest man) that shall go to deride the Being of things which a whole Countrey has now beheld. (Section XXXIII)

This vision of reality can be translated from the sphere of dogmatic religious knowledge to the realm of experimental science without a great transformation in the underlying assumption by which both are governed. The "progress" Hawthorne witnessed did not disestablish the idea of uncanny possibility, only of its cause and origin. It reshaped concepts of what the realities of life and what the possibilities of life are. Whereas traditionally supernatural causes could be supposed for natural events—old Pyncheon's death is seen to be the consequence of Maule's curse—some of the new technologies of Hawthorne's age could make what look like supernatural events have apparently natural causes.

Rappaccini's unnatural daughter is not a demon creation of a supernatural devil (even should a reader wish to interpret him as analogous to one), but the product of her father's knowledge and experiment. Chillingworth's entry into Dimmesdale soul is not wrought by witchcraft but psychological acumen. In the story "The Snow Image," the snow image is not a demon spirit but an emblem representing the spirit of a young imagination.

Hawthorne lived in an age dominated by extraordinary political, geographical and technological change. The result for the age was a sense of power derived from new victories and new accomplishments, from venturing beyond limits which had been regarded as inviolable. The American and the French Revolutions redefined not only the nature of governance or the "Rights of Man," but also the very concepts of human nature, human limits, power, and obligation. Geographical exploration brought vast areas of the world under European control. Such places, untouched by European civilization and its constructs, had previously existed only in the fantasies of writers like Montaigne when he wrote about cannibals, Shakespeare in *The Tempest*, Swift in *Gulliver's Travels*, Defoe in *Robinson Crusoe*, or Bernardin de Saint-Pierre, the author of *Paul and Virginia*.

Two months before Hawthorne's birth on July 4, 1804, Lewis and Clark had set out to explore the Louisiana Territory, just purchased from the French by President Thomas Jefferson. In 1804, too, the twelfth amendment was added to the United States Constitution. By far the longest and most legalistic to that date, and like the eleventh, but unlike the famous first ten, procedural rather than philosophical, it established the Electoral College. These coincident events serve as markers for the poles of Hawthorne's fiction, too. The conflict between exploring the unknown and imposing a controlling authority on human society, signaling the expansion and the containment of power, is a conflict between mystery and order, a conflict whose investigation pervades his work. Hawthorne's fictions, as products of their era, then can be read as hypotheses about nature, reflections on knowledge and explorations of the limits of the possible. His fiction achieves its tension through the encounter of apparently irreconcilable forces.

In the colonies of the New World, belief in the mysterious world of specters and demons, in the human capacity to wield supernatural influence, formed the accepted and acceptable way to understand phenomena and especially to hypothesize such power as witchcraft, as the Salem witch trials demonstrate. Hawthorne's fascination with the Puritan belief in a spectral world of demonic power, diabolical influence, and the possibility of one's spirit being possessed by another is the same fascination he has with the "scientific" power his creations like Rappaccini, Westerveld, Drs. Heidegger and Chillingworth practice.

In *The House of the Seven Gables*, Hawthorne writes about both periods and both versions of power. The period of the patriarch Colonel Pyncheon was that same Puritan time that saw Hawthorne's grandfather, John Hathorne, accuse some of his townsfolk of being witches and condemn them to death. It is precisely what Colonel Pyncheon did to Matthew Maule, in *The House of the Seven Gables*, in order to obtain the land that had been Maule's so he could build the house of the book's title for himself and the Pyncheon posterity. With the house, he bequeathed old Maule's blood curse, and his descendents' desire for justice. The novel introduces not only the invisible world of electric power. It accepts the Puritan belief in evil spirits, bewitchment, and the power of one person to control another. It contrasts to those demonic powers the intrusive power of wealth, station and property. By the exercise of legal and economic power, Colonel Pyncheon and, historically, the people of Salem, exercised a life and death rule over others. The counter exercise of the power of spectral or psychological influence is represented as either diabolic or "scientific." In *The House of the Seven Gables* both forms are practiced, first as a blood curse and then as mesmerism in retaliation for legal and economic wrongs.

In *The House of the Seven Gables*, through the vehicle of a feud between two families and their exchange of injuries, Hawthorne explores not only the interaction and effect of material and spiritual power but the impulse of one person to exercise domination over another. This is a recurring theme for Hawthorne, recognizable from *The Scarlet Letter*, and provides the substance of many of Hawthorne's tales. Roger Chillingworth is one of many figures in Hawthorne's fiction who pursue the arts and crafts of secret knowledge in an attempt to tamper with life and to achieve dominion over it and over others. Hawthorne's characterization of Chillingworth's motives as going beyond jealousy and vengeance and becoming a malignancy growing out of his motive— but now independent of them—casts light on others like him in Hawthorne's work who are without his motives.

Old Roger Chillingworth, throughout life, had been calm in temperament, kindly, though not of warm affections, but ever, and in all his relations with the world, a pure and upright man. He had begun an investigation, as he imagined, with the severe and equal integrity of a judge, desirous only of truth, even as if the question ... [did not involve] ... human passions, and wrongs inflicted on himself. But, as he proceeded, *a terrible fascination, a kind of fierce, though still calm, necessity seized the old man within its gripe, and never set him free again, until he had done all its bidding.* (133) (Emphasis added.)

Being in the grip of inquiry so strongly that he loses sight of the person through or upon whom he is conducting the inquiry—quite independently of any motive—and being obsessed by a fixed idea signify the "devil's work" that engages Chillingworth. Inquiry, experiment, science, for those like Chillingworth, are servants of domination. Pursuing them more deliberately than retaining a devotion to another person's integrity is the error of nearly all of Hawthorne's experimenters. It is what Hawthorne calls, in "Ethan Brand," the "Unpardonable Sin." It is a sin of men obsessed by their schemes and visions and who can therefore deny the nature or humanity of the people with whom they engage for the sake of exercising their power and accomplishing their will. This cold and obsessive devotion to an idea is, as Hawthorne shows in Governor Endicott's confrontation with the bride and groom in "The Maypole of Merry Mount," the driving force of Puritanism. And it is the driving force of the protagonists of stories like "The Birthmark," "Dr. Heidegger's Experiment," "The Snow Image," and "Rappaccini's Daughter," as well as the novels.

Hawthorne's work often shows power as the aim of men devoted to imposing their wills upon a world they see as imperfect and uncongenial in its design, which they attempt to shape to their own vision. It is an extension of the Puritan attitude and doctrine of constraining humanity and asserting the discipline of the whipping post against the freedom of the Maypole, of imagining a human power superior to nature's, able to manipulate and control it.

Mesmerism, or hypnosis, is a version of this power which appears repeatedly and disturbingly in Hawthorne's fiction. It represents an intense attack upon the person of the subject that renders her no longer her own, but the helpless creature of another robbed of her own will and humanity. In The *House of the Seven Gables* hypnotism is the instrument of vengeance taken by one of Maule's descendents who destroys Alice Pyncheon after being scorned by her father. It is Holgrave's renunciation of mesmerism generations later when he has Phoebe Pyncheon in his power as his ancestor held Alice Pyncheon in his, and might revenge the Maules, that signals the triumph of love over power and facilitates reconciliation between Pyncheons and Maules.

"The miraculous power of one human being over the will and passions of another...." (*Blithedale Romance*, 183) is the element which makes mesmerism both fascinating and repulsive to Hawthorne. In its essence this is the same force as sexual power. The identity is openly proclaimed in *The House of the Seven Gables* in both its tales of hypnosis. It is also the conclusion the reader is drawn to in *The Marble Faun*. Donatello commits murder in response to the influence of Miriam's glance. Hypnosis is of key significance in *The Blithedale Romance*, where both Westervelt, the mesmerist, and Hollingsworth, his equal in persuasive power because of a dominating personality, command the will of Priscilla. In a letter written from Brook Farm—which was the model for the community described in *The Blithedale Romance*—dated October 18, 1841, to Sophia, whom he called his wife even before their marriage, he cautions her regarding her desire to undergo mesmeric influence to alleviate recurring headaches. Speaking to her of "these magnetic miracles," he "beseech[es]" her "to take no part in them." Using language rich in sexual imagery, he argues:

> If I possessed such a power over thee, I should dare not exercise it; nor can I consent to its being exercised by another. Supposing that this power arises from the transfusion of one spirit into another, it seems to me that the sacredness of an individual; is violated by it; there would be an intrusion into thy holy of holies—and the intruder would not be thy husband! Canst thou think, without a shrinking of thy soul, of any human being coming into closer communion with thee than I may?—than either nature or my own sense of right would permit me? I cannot. (*Blithdale Romance*, 242).

The fear of witchcraft that tormented his ancestors is characterized by the anxiety resulting from one person's ability to undermine another and gain a dominant place in his or her constitution despite the other's will. The power actualizes itself in Hawthorne's thought and fiction as a sexual terror and is accomplished through hypnotic influence. The practice of mesmerism thus indicates a failure of love and the triumph of power. So does the broader attempt at affecting the laws of nature through the sort of magical intervention that characterizes the labors of Rappaccini, Aylmer, or Dr. Heidegger. It indicates a discontent and disgust with the created world that not only indicates hubris and a subtle contempt, but generally has fatal consequences. Its practitioners are men who dwell in "an infinite, shivering solitude," who "cannot come close enough to human beings to be warmed by them," and whom Hawthorne characterizes as "individuals ajar with the world." (*The Marble Faun*, 113) This desperate isolation Hawthorne ascribes to "any accident, misfortune, crime, or peculiarity of character." It is an impulse to dominate the processes and variety of the world by the imposition of a spurious and perverse perfection through a science that seeks to control nature and people. Hawthorne characterizes it as "[t]he Unpardonable Sin ... a want of love and reverence for the Human Soul." (*BR*, 242) In Jaffrey Pyncheon's death scene, the narrator's mesmeric narrative repetitions and his catalogue of all the things which once Jaffrey coveted for his grandeur but now have not the power to make him bestir himself turn a grim gothic feature into an ironic sermon on the vanity of human power.

## IV. VEILS

For a people descended from Puritanism, the new age introduced anew the challenge of determining not only what was possible, but what was permitted or forbidden. In a literature as concerned with the tension between the permissible and the forbidden, as Hawthorne's is, it seems appropriate that one of its recurrent emblems is the veil. The contradictory properties of a veil is that it simultaneously hides and reveals, hiding the thing which it reveals by the gesture of hiding.

The Reverend Mr. Hooper begins one day, in "The Minister's Black Veil," to cover his face, never again to show it. The implication of the veil is that something deeply within himself, and, by implication, at

the center of others too, is so terrible, it must be hidden. Thereby he
unveils a pervasive attitude of gloom and human isolation which he
presents to his entire congregation. His gesture is the loudest sermon
against being comfortable with the things of this world he could deliver.
At his death, he makes these things clear:

> "Why do you tremble at me alone?" cried he, turning his
> veiled face round the circle of pale spectators. "Tremble also
> at each other! Have men avoided me, and women shown no
> pity, and children screamed and fled, only for my black veil?
> What, but the mystery which it obscurely typifies, has made
> this piece of crape so awful? When the friend shows his
> innermost heart to his friend; the lover to his best beloved;
> when man does not shrink from the eye of his creator,
> loathsomely treasuring up the secret of his sin; then deem me
> a monster, for the symbol beneath which I have lived, and
> die! I look around me, and, lo! On every visage a Black Veil!"

In *The House of the Seven Gables*, "The Prophetic Pictures," and
"Edward Randolph's Picture," portraits are kept behind veils until what
is painted in them reveals itself to the characters in the story, usually as
their hidden destiny. The story of the "Veiled Lady" in *The Blithedale
Romance* is narrated first as if it were an interpolated tale, behind a veil
itself, rather than integral to the main plot which is also presented as if
obscured rather than directly. By reason of her veil "She beholds the
absolute," says Westervelt, who controls her. Being hidden herself, she
uncovers things for others. Priscilla is as much veiled by the power of
mesmerism as by the silks of her stage attire, showing mesmerism to be
a kind of veil itself, separating the person from self-knowledge and
autonomy. (186)

Miriam, in *The Marble Faun*, is a veiled figure, mysteriously
pursued by a mysterious persecutor and a by past of mysterious incidents
unknown to the reader although we see their present consequences. The
oblique structure of the narrative itself and its selective withholding of
information—keeping the specific nature of her tormentor's hold over
Miriam veiled and unclear, suggesting sexual, psychological, mesmeric
or violent origins—makes a kind of veil behind which the novel's action
occurs. Both Miriam and Donatello, faun-like at the start, in the course

of the novel become literally veiled when they cover themselves, in penitential recognition of a shattering shared guilt, which, through a murder, unites them in a mutual sexual-like ecstasy which also repels them. Frequently in his work Hawthorne constructs frames around the central tale causing the story to appear to be coming from behind a veil, of time or memory or mystery as in so many of the *Twice Told Tales*. Even *The Scarlet Letter* is distanced by "The Custom House," in which Hawthorne reveals the hidden manuscript behind his own recreation of that manuscript. Stories like the four which comprise "Legends of the Province House," are presented as one narrator's narrative of another narrator's stories coming from the Republic's colonial past.

In the preface to *The Marble Faun* Hawthorne speaks, in what is to be taken as his own voice, and then "retire[s] behind the curtain," momentarily unveiling himself, but thereby suggesting that the entire romance veils him. In 1840, in a letter to Sophia, he had written "that words may be a thick and darksome veil of mystery between the soul and the truth which it seeks." (Moore, et al, xi) Hawthorne's tales are often constructed to suggest that they are narratives veiled by something in the structure of the narrative itself. In *The Blithedale Romance* Miles Coverdale is at the center of the action, only because he narrates *The Blithedale Romance*. From the point of view of any of the other characters, he is quite peripheral.

## CODA

Homiletic tales, characterized by veiled meanings and by emblems, Hawthorne's stories examine social, spiritual, and psychological quests and struggles. They tell of people torn between conflicting desires and contradictory demands, between innocence and experience, between sin and virtue, between delight and despair. They are meditations on the proper limits and possibilities of both knowledge and power, and they chart the varieties and the nature of human association and perception. As an artist Hawthorne effected a transmutation in his source material. Gathered from a stern and moralistic culture, his stories show deep concern for moral issues. Nevertheless, the stories are ambiguous rather than apodictic, aesthetic rather than didactic. Therefore, they are not burdened by the austerity and the gloom they chronicle. Hawthorne, as artist, is a conscious and chastened version of those mesmeric intruders

into other people's souls and those maniacs who attempt to transform
the nature of reality by their secret arts, of whom he writes. Hawthorne
remains behind the veil of words he weaves, transforming that austere
symbol of hidden things—the veil—into literature, revealing not only
antinomies, torments, and struggles but the beauty of the veil itself, its
suggestiveness, the art of its weave and design, the sensuousness of its
texture.

## WORKS CITED

Fletcher, Angus. *Allegory: The Theory of A Symbolic Mode.* Ithaca: Cornell
University Press, pp. 82–83.

Hawthorne, Nathaniel. "The Threefold Destiny." In *Twice Told Tales.*
Pleasantvile, N.Y.: The Reader's Digest Association, 1989, p. 322.

———. *The Scarlet Letter.* New York: Everyman's Library/Alfred A.
Knopf, p. 10.

———. The Letters, 1843–1853, edited by Thomas Wilson, L. Neal
Smith, and Norman Holmes. Pearson. Ohio State University
Press, 1985, p. 307.

———. "Ethan Brand." In *The Celestial Railroad and Other Stories.* New
York: Signet/The New American Library, 1963, p. 280.

———. *The House of the Seven Gables.* New York: Signet/The New
American Library, 1961, p. 230.

———. "Hawthorne's Attitude Toward Mesmerism." In *The Blithedale
Romance,* New York: W.W. Norton & Company, 1978, p. 242.

———. *The Marble Faun Or, The Romance of Monte Beni.* Ohio State
University Press, 1968, p. 113.

James, Henry. *Hawthorne.* New York: Harper & Brothers, 1880, pp.
57–58.

Marx, Leo. "Forward." In *The Scarlet Letter.* New York: Signet/The New
American Library, p. xi.

Moore, Thomas R. *A Thick and Darksome Veil: The Rhetoric of
Hawthorne's Sketches, Prefaces, and Essays.* Boston: Northeastern
University Press, 1994, p.xi.

HENRY JAMES

# Early Writings

The second volume of the *Twice-Told Tales* was published in 1845, in Boston; and at this time a good many of the stories which were afterwards collected into the *Mosses from an Old Manse* had already appeared, chiefly in *The Democratic Review*, a sufficiently flourishing periodical of that period. In mentioning these things, I anticipate; but I touch upon the year 1845 in order to speak of the two collections of *Twice-Told Tales* at once. During the same year Hawthorne edited an interesting volume, the *Journals of an African Cruiser*, by his friend Bridge, who had gone into the Navy and seen something of distant waters. His biographer mentions that even then Hawthorne's name was thought to bespeak attention for a book, and he insists on this fact in contradiction to the idea that his productions had hitherto been as little noticed as his own declaration that he remained "for a good many years the obscurest man of letters in America," might lead one, and has led many people, to suppose. "In this dismal chamber FAME was won," he writes in Salem, in 1836. And we find in the Note-Books (1840) this singularly beautiful and touching passage:—

> "Here I sit in my old accustomed chamber, where I used
> to sit in days gone by.... Here I have written many tales—
> many that have been burned to ashes, many that have

From *Hawthorne* by Henry James. © 1880 by Harper & Brothers, Publishers. Reprinted by permission.

doubtless deserved the same fate. This claims to be called a haunted chamber, for thousands upon thousands of visions have appeared to me in it; and some few of them have become visible to the world. If ever I should have a biographer, he ought to make great mention of this chamber in my memoirs, because so much of my lonely youth was wasted here, and here my mind and character were formed; and here I have been glad and hopeful, and here I have been despondent. And here I sat a long, long time, waiting patiently for the world to know me, and sometimes wondering why it did not know me sooner, or whether it would ever know me at all—at least till I were in my grave. And sometimes it seems to me as if I were already in the grave, with only life enough to be chilled and benumbed. But oftener I was happy—at least as happy as I then knew how to be, or was aware of the possibility of being. By and by the world found me out in my lonely chamber, and called me forth—not, indeed, with a loud roar of acclamation, but rather with a still small voice—and forth I went, but found nothing in the world I thought preferable to my solitude till now.... And now I begin to understand why I was imprisoned so many years in this lonely chamber, and why I could never break through the viewless bolts and bars; for if I had sooner made my escape into the world, I should have grown hard and rough and been covered with earthly dust, and my heart might have become callous by rude encounters with the multitude.... But living in solitude till the fulness of time was come, I still kept the dew of my youth and the freshness of my heart.... I used to think that I could imagine all passions, all feelings, and states of the heart and mind; but how little did I know? ... Indeed, we are but shadows: we are not endowed with real life, and all that seems most real about us is but the thinnest substance of a dream—till the heart be touched. That touch creates us—then we begin to be— thereby we are beings of reality and inheritors of eternity."

There is something exquisite in the soft philosophy of this little retrospect, and it helps us to appreciate it to know that the writer had at this time just become engaged to be married to a charming and accomplished person, with whom his union, which took place two years later, was complete and full of happiness. But I quote it more particularly for the evidence it affords that, already in 1840, Hawthorne could speak of the world finding him out and calling him forth, as of an event tolerably well in the past. He had sent the first of the *Twice-Told* series to his old college friend, Longfellow, who had already laid, solidly, the foundation of his great poetic reputation, and at the time of his sending it had written him a letter from which it will be to our purpose to quote a few lines:—

"You tell me you have met with troubles and changes. I know not what these may have been: but I can assure you that trouble is the next best thing to enjoyment, and that there is no fate in the world so horrible as to have no share in either its joys or sorrows. For the last ten years I have not lived, but only dreamed of living. It may be true that there may have been some unsubstantial pleasures here in the shade, which I might have missed in the sunshine, but you cannot conceive how utterly devoid of satisfaction all my retrospects are. I have laid up no treasure of pleasant remembrances against old age; but there is some comfort in thinking that future years may be more varied, and therefore more tolerable, than the past. You give me more credit than I deserve in supposing that I have led a studious life. I have indeed turned over a good many books, but in so desultory a way that it cannot be called study, nor has it left me the fruits of study.... I have another great difficulty in the lack of materials; for I have seen so little of the world that I have nothing but thin air to concoct my stories of, and it is not easy to give a life-like semblance to such shadowy stuff. Sometimes, through a peephole, I have caught a glimpse of the real world, and the two or three articles in which I have portrayed these glimpses please me better than the others."

It is more particularly for the sake of the concluding lines that I have quoted this passage; for evidently no portrait of Hawthorne at this period is at all exact which fails to insist upon the constant struggle which must have gone on between his shyness and his desire to know something of life; between what may be called his evasive and his inquisitive tendencies. I suppose it is no injustice to Hawthorne to say that, on the whole, his shyness always prevailed; and yet, obviously, the struggle was constantly there. He says of his *Twice-Told Tales*, in the preface, "They are not the talk of a secluded man with his own mind and heart (had it been so they could hardly have failed to be more deeply and permanently valuable,) but his attempts, and very imperfectly successful ones, to open an intercourse with the world." We are speaking here of small things, it must be remembered—of little attempts, little sketches, a little world. But everything is relative, and this smallness of scale must not render less apparent the interesting character of Hawthorne's efforts. As for the *Twice-Told Tales* themselves, they are an old story now; every one knows them a little, and those who admire them particularly have read them a great many times. The writer of this sketch belongs to the latter class, and he has been trying to forget his familiarity with them, and ask himself what impression they would have made upon him at the time they appeared, in the first bloom of their freshness, and before the particular Hawthorne-quality, as it may be called, had become an established, a recognised and valued, fact. Certainly I am inclined to think, if one had encountered these delicate, dusky flowers in the blossomless garden of American journalism, one would have plucked them with a very tender hand; one would have felt that here was something essentially fresh and new; here, in no extraordinary force or abundance, but in a degree distinctly appreciable, was an original element in literature. When I think of it, I almost envy Hawthorne's earliest readers; the sensation of opening upon *The Great Carbuncle, The Seven Vagabonds*, or *The Threefold Destiny* in an American annual of forty years ago, must have been highly agreeable.

Among these shorter things (it is better to speak of the whole collection, including the *Snow Image* and the *Mosses from an Old Manse*, at once) there are three sorts of tales, each one of which has an original stamp. There are, to begin with, the stories of fantasy and allegory— those among which the three I have just mentioned would be numbered, and which, on the whole, are the most original. This is the group to which such little masterpieces as *Malvin's Burial, Rappacini's Daughter*, and *Young Goodman Brown* also belong—these two last perhaps representing the highest point that Hawthorne reached in this direction.

Then there are the little tales of New England history, which are scarcely less admirable, and of which *The Grey Champion*, *The Maypole of Merry Mount*, and the four beautiful *Legends of the Province House*, as they are called, are the most successful specimens. Lastly come the slender sketches of actual scenes and of the objects and manners about him, by means of which, more particularly, he endeavoured "to open an intercourse with the world," and which, in spite of their slenderness, have an infinite grace and charm. Among these things *A Bill from the Town Pump*, *The Village Uncle*, *The Toll-Gatherer's Day*, the *Chippings with a Chisel*, may most naturally be mentioned. As we turn over these volumes we feel that the pieces that spring most directly from his fancy constitute, as I have said (putting his four novels aside), his most substantial claim to our attention. It would be a mistake to insist too much upon them; Hawthorne was himself the first to recognise that. "These fitful sketches," he says in the preface to the *Mosses from an Old Manse*, "with so little of external life about them, yet claiming no profundity of purpose—so reserved even while they sometimes seem so frank—often but half in earnest, and never, even when most so, expressing satisfactorily the thoughts which they profess to image—such trifles, I truly feel, afford no solid basis for a literary reputation." This is very becomingly uttered; but it may be said, partly in answer to it, and partly in confirmation, that the valuable element in these things was not what Hawthorne put into them consciously, but what passed into them without his being able to measure it—the element of simple genius, the quality of imagination. This is the real charm of Hawthorne's writing—this purity and spontaneity and naturalness of fancy. For the rest, it is interesting to see how it borrowed a particular colour from the other faculties that lay near it—how the imagination, in this capital son of the old Puritans, reflected the hue of the more purely moral part, of the dusky, overshadowed conscience. The conscience, by no fault of its own, in every genuine offshoot of that sombre lineage, lay under the shadow of the sense of *sin*. This darkening cloud was no essential part of the nature of the individual; it stood fixed in the general moral heaven under which he grew up and looked at life. It projected from above, from outside, a black patch over his spirit, and it was for him to do what he could with the black patch. There were all sorts of possible ways of dealing with it; they depended upon the personal temperament. Some natures would let it lie as it fell, and contrive to be tolerably comfortable beneath it. Others would groan and sweat and suffer; but the dusky blight would remain, and their lives would be lives of misery. Here and there an individual, irritated beyond endurance, would throw it off in anger, plunging probably into what would be deemed deeper abysses of depravity. Hawthorne's way was the best; for he contrived, by an exquisite process, best known to himself, to transmute this heavy moral burden into the very substance of the imagination, to make it evaporate in the light and charming fumes of artistic production. But Hawthorne, of course, was exceptionally fortunate; he had his genius to help him. Nothing is more curious and interesting than this almost exclusively *imported* character of the sense of sin in Hawthorne's mind; it seems to exist there merely for an artistic or literary purpose. He had ample cognizance of the Puritan conscience; it was his natural heritage; it was reproduced in him; looking into his soul, he found it there. But his relation to it was only, as one may say, intellectual; it was not moral and theological. He played with it, and used it as a pigment; he treated it, as the metaphysicians say, objectively. He was not discomposed, disturbed, haunted by it, in the manner of its usual and regular victims, who had not the little postern door of fancy to slip through, to the other side of the wall. It was, indeed, to his imaginative vision, the great fact of man's nature; the light element that had been mingled with his own composition always clung to this rugged prominence of moral responsibility, like the mist that hovers about the mountain. It was a necessary condition for a man of Hawthorne's stock that if his imagination should take license to amuse itself, it should at least select this grim precinct of the Puritan morality for its play-ground. He speaks of the dark disapproval with which his old ancestors, in the case of their coming to life, would see him trifling himself away as a story-teller. But how far more darkly would they have frowned could they have understood that he had converted the very principle of their own being into one of his toys!

It will be seen that I am far from being struck with the justice of that view of the author of the *Twice-Told Tales*, which is so happily expressed by the French critic to whom I alluded at an earlier stage of this essay. To speak of Hawthorne, as M. Emile Montégut does, as a *romancier pessimiste*, seems to me very much beside the mark. He is no more a pessimist than an optimist, though he is certainly not much of either. He does not pretend to conclude, or to have a philosophy of human nature; indeed, I should even say that at bottom be does not take human nature as hard as be may seem to do. "His bitterness," says M. Montégut, "is without abatement, and his bad opinion of man is without compensation.... His little tales have the air of confessions which the soul makes to itself; they are so many little slaps which the author applies to our face." This, it seems to me, is to exaggerate almost immeasurably the reach of Hawthorne's relish of gloomy subjects. What pleased him in such subjects was their picturesqueness, their rich duskiness of colour, their chiaroscuro; but they were not the expression of a hopeless, or even of a predominantly melancholy, feeling about the human soul. Such at least is my own impression. He is to a considerable degree ironical—this is part of his charm—part even, one may say, of his brightness; but he is neither bitter nor cynical—he is rarely even what I should call tragical. There have certainly been story-tellers of a gayer and lighter spirit; there have been observers more humorous, more hilarious—though on the whole Hawthorne's observation has a smile in it oftener than may at first appear; but there has rarely been an observer more serene, less agitated by what he sees and less disposed to call things deeply into question. As I have already intimated, his Note-Books are full of this simple and almost childlike serenity. That dusky pre-occupation with the misery of human life and the wickedness of the human heart which such a critic as M. Emile Montégut talks about, is totally absent from them; and if we may suppose a person to have read these Diaries before looking into the tales, we may be sure that such a reader would be greatly surprised to hear the author described as a disappointed, disdainful genius. "This marked love of cases of conscience," says M. Montégut; "this taciturn, scornful cast of mind; this habit of seeing sin everywhere, and hell always gaping open; this dusky gaze bent always upon a damned world, and a nature draped in mourning; these lonely conversations of the imagination with the conscience; this pitiless analysis resulting from a perpetual examination of one's self, and from the tortures of a heart closed before men and open to God—all these elements of the Puritan character have passed into Mr. Hawthorne, or, to speak more justly, have *filtered* into him, through a long succession of generations." This is a very pretty and very vivid account of Hawthorne, superficially considered; and it is just such a view of the case as would commend itself most easily and most naturally to a hasty critic. It is all true indeed, with a difference; Hawthorne was all that M. Montégut says, minus the conviction. The old Puritan moral sense, the consciousness of sin and hell, of the fearful nature of our responsibilities and the savage character of our Taskmaster—these things had been lodged in the mind of a man of Fancy, whose fancy had straightway begun to take liberties and play tricks with them—to judge them (Heaven forgive him!) from the poetic and aesthetic point of view, the point of view of entertainment and irony. This absence of conviction makes the difference; but the difference is great.

Hawthorne was a man of fancy, and I suppose that, in speaking of him, it is inevitable that we should feel ourselves confronted with the familiar problem of the difference between the fancy and the imagination. Of the larger and more potent faculty he certainly possessed a liberal share; no one can read *The House of the Seven Gables* without feeling it to be a deeply imaginative work. But I am often struck, especially in the shorter tales, of which I am now chiefly speaking, with a kind of small ingenuity, a taste for conceits and analogies, which bears more particularly what is called the fanciful stamp. The finer of the shorter tales are redolent of a rich imagination.

> "Had Goodman Brown fallen asleep in the forest and only dreamed a wild dream of witch-meeting? Be it so, if you will; but, alas, it was a dream of evil omen for young Goodman Brown! a stern, a sad, a darkly meditative, a distrustful, if not a desperate, man, did he become from the night of that fearful dream. On the Sabbath-day, when the congregation were singing a holy psalm, he could not listen, because an anthem of sin rushed loudly upon his ear and drowned all the blessed strain. When the minister spoke from the pulpit, with power and fervid eloquence, and with his hand on the open Bible of the sacred truth of our religion, and of saint-like lives and triumphant deaths, and of future bliss or misery unutterable, then did Goodman Brown grow pale, dreading lest the roof should thunder down upon the gray blasphemer and his hearers. Often, awaking suddenly at midnight, he shrank from the bosom of Faith; and at morning or eventide, when the family knelt down at prayer, he scowled and muttered to himself, and gazed sternly at his wife, and turned away. And when he had lived long, and was borne to his grave

a hoary corpse, followed by Faith, an aged woman, and children, and grandchildren, a goodly procession, besides neighbours not a few, they carved no hopeful verse upon his tombstone, for his dying hour was gloom."

There is imagination in that, and in many another passage that I might quote; but as a general thing I should characterise the more metaphysical of our author's short stories as graceful and felicitous conceits. They seem to me to be qualified in this manner by the very fact that they belong to the province of allegory. Hawthorne, in his metaphysical moods, is nothing if not allegorical, and allegory, to my sense, is quite one of the lighter exercises of the imagination. Many excellent judges, I know, have a great stomach for it; they delight in symbols and correspondences, in seeing a story told as if it were another and a very different story. I frankly confess that I have, as a general thing, but little enjoyment of it, and that it has never seemed to me to be, as it were, a first-rate literary form. It has produced assuredly some first-rate works; and Hawthorne in his younger years had been a great reader and devotee of Bunyan and Spenser, the great masters of allegory. But it is apt to spoil two good things—a story and a moral, a meaning and a form; and the taste for it is responsible for a large part of the forcible-feeble writing that has been inflicted upon the world. The only cases in which it is endurable is when it is extremely spontaneous, when the analogy presents itself with eager promptitude. When it shows signs of having been groped and fumbled for, the needful illusion is of course absent, and the failure complete. Then the machinery alone is visible, and the end to which it operates becomes a matter of indifference. There was but little literary criticism in the United States at the time Hawthorne's earlier works were published; but among the reviewers Edgar Poe perhaps held the scales the highest. He, at any rate, rattled the loudest, and pretended, more than any one else, to conduct the weighing-process on scientific principles. Very remarkable was this process of Edgar Poe's, and very extraordinary were his principles; but he had the advantage of being a man of genius, and his intelligence was frequently great. His collection of critical sketches of the American writers flourishing in what M. Taine would call his *milieu* and *moment*, is very curious and interesting reading, and it has one quality which ought to keep it from ever being completely forgotten. It is probably the most complete and exquisite specimen of *provincialism* ever prepared for the edification of men. Poe's judgments are pretentious, spiteful, vulgar; but they contain a great deal of sense and discrimination as well, and here and there, sometimes at frequent intervals, we find a phrase of happy insight imbedded in a patch of the most fatuous pedantry. He wrote a chapter upon Hawthorne, and spoke of him, on the whole, very kindly; and his estimate is of sufficient value to make it noticeable that he should express lively disapproval of the large part allotted to allegory in his tales—in defence of which, he says, "however, or for whatever object employed, there is scarcely one respectable word to be said.... The deepest emotion," he goes on, "aroused within us by the happiest allegory *as* allegory, is a very, *very* imperfectly satisfied sense of the writer's ingenuity in overcoming a difficulty we should have preferred his not having attempted to overcome.... One thing is clear, that if allegory ever establishes a fact, it is by dint of overturning a fiction;" and Poe has furthermore the courage to remark that the *Pilgrim's Progress* is a "ludicrously overrated book." Certainly, as a general thing, we are struck with the ingenuity and felicity of Hawthorne's analogies and correspondences; the idea appears to have made itself at home in them easily. Nothing could be better in this respect than *The Snow Image* (a little masterpiece), or *The Great Carbuncle*, or *Doctor Heidegger's Experiment*, or *Rappacini's Daughter*. But in such things as *The Birth-Mark* and *The Bosom-Serpent* we are struck with something stiff and mechanical, slightly incongruous, as if the kernel had not assimilated its envelope. But these are matters of light impression, and there would be a want of tact in pretending to discriminate too closely among things which all, in one way or another, have a charm. The charm—the great charm—is that they are glimpses of a great field, of the whole deep mystery of man's soul and conscience. They are moral, and their interest is moral; they deal with something more than the mere accidents and conventionalities, the surface occurrences of life. The fine thing in Hawthorne is that he cared for the deeper psychology, and that in his way, he tried to become familiar with it. This natural, yet fanciful, familiarity with it; this air, on the author's part, of being a confirmed *habitué* of a region of mysteries and subtleties, constitutes the originality of his tales. And then they have the further merit of seeming, for what they are, to spring up so freely and lightly. The author has all the ease, indeed, of a regular dweller in the moral, psychological realm; he goes to and fro in it, as a man who knows his way. His tread is a light and modest one, but he keeps the key in his pocket.

His little historical stories all seem to me admirable; they are so good that you may re-read them many times. They are not numerous, and they are very short; but they are full of a vivid and delightful sense of the New England past; they have, moreover, the distinction, little tales of a dozen and fifteen pages as they are, of being the only successful attempts at historical fiction that have been made in the United States. Hawthorne was at home in the early Now England history; he had thumbed its records and he had breathed its air, in whatever odd receptacles this somewhat pungent compound still lurked. He was fond of it, and he was proud of it, as any Now Englander must be, measuring the part of that handful of half-starved fanatics who formed his earliest precursors, in laying the foundations of a mighty empire. Hungry for the picturesque as he always was, and not finding any very copious provision of it around him, he turned back into the two preceding centuries, with the earnest determination that the primitive annals of Massachusetts should at least appear picturesque. His fancy, which was always alive, played a little with the somewhat meagre and angular facts of the colonial period, and forthwith converted a great many of them into impressive legends and pictures. There is a little infusion of colour, a little vagueness about certain details, but it is very gracefully and discreetly done, and realities are kept in view sufficiently to make us feel that if we are reading romance, it is romance that rather supplements than contradicts history. The early annals of New England were not fertile in legend, but Hawthorne laid his hands upon everything that would serve his purpose, and in two or three cases his version of the story has a great deal of beauty. *The Gray Champion* is a sketch of less than eight pages, but the little figures stand up in the tale as stoutly, at the least, as if they were propped up on half-a-dozen chapters by a dryer annalist; and the whole thing has the merit of those cabinet pictures in which the artist has been able to make his persons look the size of life. Hawthorne, to say it again, was not in the least a realist—he was not to my mind enough of one; but there is no genuine lover of the good city of Boston but will feel grateful to him for his courage in attempting to recount the "traditions" of Washington Street, the main thoroughfare of the Puritan capital. The four *Legends of the Province House* are certain shadowy stories which he professes to have gathered in an ancient tavern lurking behind the modern shop fronts of this part of the city. The Province House disappeared some years ago, but while it stood it was pointed to as the residence of the Royal Governors of Massachusetts before the Revolution. I have no recollection of it; but it cannot have been, even from Hawthorne's account of it—which is as pictorial as he ventures to make it—a very imposing piece of antiquity. The writer's charming touch, however, throws a rich brown tone over its rather shallow venerableness; and we are beguiled into believing, for instance, at the close of *Howe's Masquerade* (a story of a strange occurrence at an entertainment given by Sir William Howe, the last of the Royal Governors, during the siege of Boston by Washington), that "superstition, among other legends of this mansion, repeats the wondrous tale that on the anniversary night of Britain's discomfiture the ghosts of the ancient governors of Massachusetts still glide through the Province House. And last of all comes a figure shrouded in a military cloak, tossing his clenched hands into the air, and stamping his iron-shod boots upon the freestone steps with a semblance of feverish despair, but without the sound of a foot-tramp." Hawthorne had, as regards the two earlier centuries of New England life, that faculty which is called now-a-days the historic consciousness. He never sought to exhibit it on a large scale; he exhibited it, indeed, on a scale so minute that we must not linger too much upon it. His vision of the past was filled with definite images—images none the less definite that they were concerned with events as shadowy as this dramatic passing away of the last of King George's representatives in his long loyal but finally alienated colony.

I have said that Hawthorne had become engaged in about his thirty-fifth year; but he was not married until 1842. Before this event took place he passed through two episodes, which (putting his falling in love aside) were much the most important things that had yet happened to him. They interrupted the painful monotony of his life, and brought the affairs of men within his personal experience. One of these was, moreover, in itself a curious and interesting chapter of observation, and it fructified, in Hawthorne's memory, in one of his best productions. How urgently he needed at this time to be drawn within the circle of social accidents, a little anecdote related by Mr. Lathrop in connection with his first acquaintance with the young lady he was to marry, may serve as an example. This young lady became known to him through her sister, who had first approached him as an admirer of the *Twice-Told Tales* (as to the authorship of which she had been so much in the dark as to have attributed it first, conjecturally, to one of the two Miss Hathornes); and the two Miss Peabodys, desiring to see more of the charming writer, caused him to be invited to a species of *conversazione* at the house of one of their friends, at which they themselves took care to be punctual. Several other ladies, however, were as punctual as they, and Hawthorne presently arriving, and seeing a bevy of admirers where he had expected but three or four, fell into a state of agitation, which is vividly described by his biographer. He "stood perfectly motionless, but with the look of a sylvan creature on the point of fleeing away.... He was stricken with dismay; his face lost colour and took on a warm paleness, ... his agitation was very great; he stood by a table, and, taking up some small object that lay upon it, he found his hand trembling so that he was obliged to lay it down." It was desirable, certainly, that something should occur to break the spell of a diffidence that might justly be called morbid. There is another little sentence dropped by Mr. Lathrop in relation to this period of Hawthorne's life, which appears to me worth quoting, though I am by no means sure that it will seem so to the reader. It has a very simple and innocent air, but to a person not without an impression of the early days of "culture" in New England it will be pregnant with historic meaning. The elder Miss Peabody, who afterwards was Hawthorne's sister-in-law, and who acquired later in life a very honourable American fame as a woman of benevolence, of learning, and of literary accomplishment, had invited the Miss Hathornes to come to her house for the evening, and to bring with them their brother, whom she wished to thank for his beautiful tales. "Entirely to her surprise," says Mr. Lathrop, completing thereby his picture of the attitude of this remarkable family toward society—"entirely to her surprise they came. She herself opened the door, and there, before her, between his sisters, stood a splendidly handsome youth, tall and strong, with no appearance whatever of timidity, but instead an almost fierce determination making his face stern. This was his resource for carrying off the extreme inward tremor which he really felt. His hostess brought out Flaxman's designs for Dante, just received from Professor Felton, of Harvard, and the party made an evening's entertainment out of them." This last sentence is the one I allude to; and were it not for fear of appearing too fanciful, I should say that these few words were, to the initiated mind, an unconscious expression of the lonely frigidity which characterised most attempts at social recreation in the New England world some forty years ago. There was at that time a great desire for culture, a great interest in knowledge, in art, in aesthetics, together with a very scanty supply of the materials for such pursuits. Small things were made to do large service; and there is something even touching in the solemnity of consideration that was bestowed by the emancipated New England conscience upon little wandering books and prints, little echoes and rumours of observation and experience. There flourished at that time in Boston a very remarkable and interesting woman, of whom we shall have more to say, Miss Margaret Fuller by name. This lady was the apostle of culture, of intellectual curiosity; and in the peculiarly interesting account of her life, published in 1852 by Emerson and two other of her friends, there are pages of her letters and diaries which narrate her visits to the Boston Athenaeum, and the emotions aroused in her mind by turning over portfolios of engravings. These emotions were ardent and passionate— could hardly have been more so had she been prostrate with contemplation in the Sistine Chapel or in one of the chambers of the Pitti Palace. The only analogy I can recall to this earnestness of interest in great works of art at a distance from them, is furnished by the great Goethe's elaborate study of plaster-casts and pencil-drawings at Weimar. I mention Margaret Fuller here because a glimpse of her state of mind— her vivacity of desire and poverty of knowledge—helps to define the situation. The situation lives for a moment in those few words of Mr. Lathrop's. The initiated mind, as I have ventured to call it, has a vision of a little unadorned parlour, with the snow-drifts of a Massachusetts winter piled up about its windows, and a group of sensitive and serious people, modest votaries of opportunity, fixing their eyes upon a bookful of Flaxman's attenuated outlines.

At the beginning of the year 1839 he received, through political interest, an appointment as weigher and gauger in the Boston Custom-house. Mr. Van Buren then occupied the Presidency, and it appears that the Democratic party, whose successful candidate he had been, rather took credit for the patronage it had bestowed upon literary men. Hawthorne was a Democrat, and, apparently a zealous one; even in later years, after the Whigs had vivified their principles by the adoption of the Republican platform, and by taking up an honest attitude on the question of slavery, his political faith never wavered. His Democratic sympathies were eminently natural, and there would have been an incongruity in his belonging to the other party. He was not only by conviction, but personally and by association, a Democrat. When in later years he found himself in contact with European civilization, he appears to have become conscious of a good deal of latent radicalism in his disposition; he was oppressed with the burden of antiquity in Europe, and he found himself sighing for lightness, and freshness and facility of change. But these things are relative to the point of view, and in his own country Hawthorne cast his lot with the party of conservatism, the party opposed to change and freshness. The people who found something musty and mouldy in his literary productions would have regarded this quite as a matter of course; but we are not obliged to use invidious epithets in describing his political preferences. The sentiment that attached him to the Democracy was a subtle and honourable one, and the author of an attempt to sketch a portrait of him should be the last to complain of this adjustment of his sympathies. It falls much more smoothly into his reader's conception of him than any other would do; and if he had had the perversity to be a Republican, I am afraid our ingenuity would have been considerably taxed in devising a proper explanation of the circumstance. At any rate, the Democrats gave him a small post in the Boston Custom-house, to which an annual salary of $1,200 was attached, and Hawthorne appears at first to have joyously welcomed the gift. The duties of the office were not very congruous to the genius of a man of fancy; but it had the advantage that it broke the spell of his cursed solitude, as he called it, drew him away from Salem, and threw him, comparatively speaking, into the world. The first volume of the American Note-Books contains some extracts from letters written during his tenure of this modest office, which indicate sufficiently that his occupations cannot have been intrinsically gratifying.

> "I have been measuring coal all day," he writes, during the winter of 1840, "on board of a black little British schooner, in a dismal dock at the north end of the city. Most of the time I paced the deck to keep myself warm; for the wind (north-east, I believe) blew up through the dock as if it had been the pipe of a pair of bellows. The vessel lying deep between two wharves, there was no more delightful prospect, on the right hand and on the left, than the posts and timbers, half

immersed in the water and covered with ice, which the rising
and falling of successive tides had left upon them, so that they
looked like immense icicles. Across the water, however, not
more than half a mile off, appeared the Bunker's Hill
Monument, and, what interested me considerably more, a
church-steeple, with the dial of a clock upon it, whereby I
was enabled to measure the march of the weary hours.
Sometimes I descended into the dirty little cabin of the
schooner, and warmed myself by a red-hot stove, among
biscuit-barrels, pots and kettles, sea-chests, and innumerable
lumber of all sorts—my olfactories meanwhile being greatly
refreshed with the odour of a pipe, which the captain, or
some one of his crew, was smoking. But at last came the
sunset, with delicate clouds, and a purple light upon the
islands; and I blessed it, because it was the signal of my
release."

A worse man than Hawthorne would have measured coal quite as
well; and of all the dismal tasks to which an unremunerated imagination
has ever had to accommodate itself, I remember none more sordid than
the business depicted in the foregoing lines. "I pray," he writes, some
weeks later, "that in one year more I may find some way of escaping from
this unblest Custom-house; for it is a very grievous thraldom. I do detest
all offices; all, at least, that are held on a political tenure, and I want
nothing to do with politicians. Their hearts wither away, and die out of
their bodies. Their consciences are turned to india-rubber, or to some
substance as black as that, and which will stretch as much. One thing, if
no more, I have gained by my Custom-house experience—to know a
politician. It is a knowledge which no previous thought or power of
sympathy could have taught me; because the animal, or the machine,
rather, is not in nature." A few days later he goes on in the same strain:—

"I do not think it is the doom laid upon me of murdering
so many of the brightest hours of the day at the Custom-
house that makes such havoc with my wits, for here I am
again trying to write worthily, ... yet with a sense as if all the
noblest part of man had been left out of my composition, or
had decayed out of it since my nature was given to my own

keeping.... Never comes any bird of Paradise into that dismal region. A salt or even a coal-ship is ten million times preferable; for there the sky is above me, and the fresh breeze around me; and my thoughts, having hardly anything to do with my occupation, are as free as air. Nevertheless ... it is only once in a while that the image and desire of a better and happier life makes me feel the iron of my chain; for after all a human spirit may find no insufficiency of food for it, even in the Custom-house. And with such materials as these I do think and feel and learn things that are worth knowing, and which I should not know unless I had learned them there; so that the present position of my life shall not be quite left out of the sum of my real existence.... It is good for me, on many accounts, that my life has had this passage in it. I know much more than I did a year ago. I have a stronger sense of power to act as a man among men. I have gained worldly wisdom, and wisdom, also, that is not altogether of this world. And when I quit this earthly career where I am now buried, nothing will cling to me that ought to be left behind. Men will not perceive, I trust, by my look, or the tenor of my thoughts and feelings, that I have been a Custom-house officer."

He says, writing shortly afterwards, that "when I shall be free again, I will enjoy all things with the fresh simplicity of a child of five years old. I shall grow young again, made all over anew. I will go forth and stand in a summer shower, and all the worldly dust that has collected on me shall be washed away at once, and my heart will be like a bank of fresh flowers for the weary to rest upon."

This forecast of his destiny was sufficiently exact. A year later, in April, 1841, he went to take up his abode in the socialistic community of Brook Farm. Here he found himself among fields and flowers and other natural products, as well as among many products that could not very justly be called natural. He was exposed to summer showers in plenty; and his personal associations were as different as possible from those he had encountered in fiscal circles. He made acquaintance with Transcendentalism and the Transcendentalists.

MICHAEL J. COLACURCIO

# "Certain Circumstances": Hawthorne and the Interest of History

I

Nothing would seem more obvious at first glance than the historical dimension of Hawthorne's literary art. His work of widest international reputation, *The Scarlet Letter*, is set squarely in the midst of the "Puritan" seventeenth century, and it shows all the signs of a determined inquiry into the moral circumstances of this relevant and specifiable past. The settings of his tales turn out to be quite various, but from among them a modest number set in colonial New England have attracted a disproportionate share of attention, as if in recognition that such "local history" were somehow his true metier. And compared to the universalism of contemporaries like Emerson and Thoreau, Hawthorne's bookish curiosity about historical particularities would certainly seem a distinguishing mark. So it might appear irresponsible to ignore the problems which arise when our literary present is constituted as an imitation of an historical past: This is now, as always, whenever anyone reads; but that was then. What if it was all different?

At the same time, however, few readers appear to relish the suggestion that what they read as "literature" may require an effort of historical reconstruction—and even of something like research. Perhaps we all begin by defining "the literary" so as to preclude that exact

From *New Essays on Hawthorne's Major Tales*, ed. Millicent Bell. © 1993 by Cambridge University Press. Reprinted with permission of Cambridge University Press.

possibility: now for something on my own terms; or else, with a little more finesse, something complete in itself, something which invents and deploys its own world of fact and assumption. Granted, all acts of writing are past to the reader; and the *further* past of historical fiction may well compound the problem of possible human difference. But all acts of reading are present; nor does literature properly speaking occur until someone actually reads. So most readers are inclined to trust their own instincts: That was then, but this is now; and life is short.

Nor have the institutions of academic criticism always opposed these readerly assumptions.[1] True, many Professors of Literature appear duty-bound to lecture their classes on something called background or context; and many of them are known to lament that teaching grows more difficult every year, as each new class seems less well informed about the history of the world where literature has been written and read.[2] But most students prove immune to this preprofessional embarrassment: They have, after all, only so much time for each course; nor did they enroll in "English" with the same factual expectations as in history or sociology. And professors usually concede the point in the end: When the push of class discussion comes to the shove of a take-home paper, any fair comment on theme or style will usually suffice. A more complex approach—more worldly or more "intertextual"—must wait till graduate school. Or for some "New Historicism," to point a way outside the well enclosed garden of literary study.[3]

Meanwhile, of the explicit "approaches" that have retarded the interest of history, one may count the discrediting effect of "source studies." In these, a scholar persuaded of the obvious—that the "Puritanism" of "Young Goodman Brown" or the revolutionary lore of "My Kinsman, Major Molineux" surely implies some special historical knowledge—sets out to locate the very books from which Hawthorne has derived his facts. Such studies have been successful in certifying an impressive number of works Hawthorne must have read. Often enough, however, historical consideration ends with the thrill of the discovery, truly electric to the investigator, but hard to communicate to the less fortunate audience. A "fact" is added to the lore of "literary history"; but the avid reader, lured to the library by the promise of insight, almost always asks, "So what?" Or else she or he is soberly instructed that, though Hawthorne has read something which *happened* to spur the creative process, he has of course gone on to "use history" for his own literary end—implying, always, that we need not trouble ourselves much about the issues of the sources themselves.[4] We honor thus the artist's creativity, but we also empower our own autonomous reading. Imagination transmutes every difficulty of worldly fact into the "textual" condition of rhetoric. A most convenient system, truly.

But another form of criticism has also acted to counter the interest of history in Hawthorne—one so habitual as to appear inevitable. Psychology may or may not appear to us as Queen of the Sciences, but whenever we sit down to read for more than mere diversion, we usually find ourselves within its quietly extensive domain; for, as serious readers, we imagine we are looking for insight into something like "the human condition"—glorious or pitiful, yet pretty much unchanged over time. Long since persuaded that the pursuit of wisdom begins nowhere but in self-knowledge, we go on to decide that literature shall be our primary aid to that reflection. Conscientiously secured and arranged by our colleges, the corpus of canonized texts represents, to us, a preserve of all the more important traits of our own curious species. Thus literature continues, without fail, to appear "more philosophical than history": It looks for evidences of things that are *always* true, about ourselves.

In loyalty to this complex of assumptions we steadfastly resist the suggestion that historical change may be real and radical—that "the self" may be largely the creation of modern ideology, and that the notion of an essential human psyche may be only a narcissistic illusion. Accordingly, in the case of Hawthorne, we seize some fragment of his language to insist that his true interest can be nothing but the profounder workings of "our common nature."[5] His characters may be Puritans or other awkward provincials but his real interests, we are sure, are timeless: not historical but human.

Predictably, therefore, critics concerned to assemble the evidence of Hawthorne's anticipations of modern psychology have worked with an agreeable sense of their own inevitability; and, happily persuaded of the primacy of their project, they have tended to mock the interest of history as merely academic.[6] Argued out in full, however, their case might demand great philosophical acumen indeed. How did we become so sure of the network of propositions that underlies our belief in "the literary" as an infallible index of "the human"? And what are the practical implications of this complex faith? May not imagination look to the condition of an historic community as well as to the structure of the psyche or the state of the soul? Must literature treat even politics as but a department of psychology?

Of course the "historicist" position is not without its own difficulties. If change is so radical a fact of human experience, how can we recover a meaningful sense of the past at all? Perhaps, on this "Heraclitan" view, its patterns of experience were so different as to escape present categories altogether. Or, to state the problem from the opposite perspective, surely we would not read *any* text if we expected to encounter an alien mentality, one that utterly eluded the scope of our own concepts. Thus a radical skepticism, very hard to reconcile with the nature of intellectual inquiry as we understand it, may lie in wait for those who would reject "essentialism" altogether. The river of thought in which we step had better be *somewhat* the same. Yet even as we are forced to accept some version of Emerson's dictum that "there is only *one mind*,"[7] we may yet resist the conclusion that psychological theory (or psychoanalytic practice) has yielded up a science of all its various moods and behaviors. And we can maintain, quite apart from questions of structure, that shifts of attention and varieties of expression are significant enough to arouse and satisfy a curiosity about human difference over time, that the writings we preserve as literature are competent to inscribe difference as well as sameness, that these two may be about equal as possible reasons to read literature.

And, finally, since readers always will, we may as well premise that they may judge for themselves: can a modest familiarity with the issues of America's colonial history offer any useful hypotheses for the interpretation of Hawthorne's early tales? If not, why have they made themselves so pedantically correct about such matters? Or if so, how may the construction of this "American Studies Hawthorne" come to modify our sense of "Hawthorne's Psychological Themes"? Perhaps these tales are trying to force us to learn something, And once we recover from the shock to our literary sensibility, we might come to like that fact.

2

One is always tempted to begin with a "Puritan" tale—the sort we associate with the "solitary" Hawthorne who, just after college, spent twelve or so years living in the home of his mother's family, reading his way through the Salem subscription library and trying (unsuccessfully) to put together several collections of tales of his "Native Land" which, however "Provincial," must yet have its own "Story."[8] From among that group, it is almost irresistibly tempting to select the widely discussed "Young Goodman Brown," which clearly invokes the (mis-)deeds of some of Hawthorne's Puritan ancestors, but also suggests other, more "profound" considerations. Yet even this prime exemplum may need to be placed within the range of Hawthorne's interest as a writer of historical fiction.

Published in 1835, after the breakup of the collection for which it was intended—and which may well have provided it with an important narrative setting—it is by no means Hawthorne's first meditation on the question of New England "witchcraft." Earlier treatments date back to his first projected collection (of 1827 or earlier) and reveal a more Gothic literary style. Clearly Hawthorne's concern was a developing one. Nor does it in any way epitomize his interest in "The Matter of Puritanism."[9] The dark mood which concludes the fictional life of Goodman Brown has often suggested some psychic kinship with the somber and solitary experience of Parson Hooper in "The Minister's Black Veil" (1836); but as Hooper's revival of Puritan gloom seems much more deliberately self-cultivated, his tale may involve other issues altogether; particularly when we learn to date its action well into the eighteenth century.[10] And elsewhere the terms are noticeably different. "The Gentle Boy" (1832) tells a sad enough story—of family disruption in the midst of sectarian dispute—but it dwells at some length on the domestic issues so popular in the fiction of the period. And a fair number of Hawthorne's Puritan tales seem not moodily spiritual at all but quite frankly *political*.

"The Gray Champion" (1835) and "Endicott and the Red Cross" (1838) both profess to find predictions of the American Revolution in acts of resistance of the most local and Puritanic sort; and even "The May-Pole of Merry Mount" (1836), often treated as a moral allegory, may fit this typological model as well as any other. When John Endicott cuts down "the only maypole in New England" (368),[11] his action may seem less political than when he rends "the Red Cross completely out of the banner" (548) of the realm of England; but only until one learns the current status of this immemorial or mythic symbol. Legitimized—even recommended by the King himself, maypole ceremonies had become, by the late 1620s, an important symbol by which England's civil religion distinguished itself from its Puritan antagonist.[12] In both cases, therefore, Endicott implies the disestablishment of an "Anglican" religion in the transatlantic territories of *New* England. And most fully evincing this care for ancestral politics, the four tales of the Revolution known as "Legends of the Province House" (1838) discover the legacy of Puritanism at work not in experiences of dark moral privacy but in a rhetoric of resistance and destiny.

The distinguishing mark of "My Kinsman, Major Molineux" (1832), in this context, is that it is frankly political without being very noticeably "Puritan." Few readers can resist its implication of interest in the American Revolution, but its point of literal reference is in fact the 1730s. And its way of being "proleptic" is not quite like that of "The Gray Champion" or "Endicott": what it offers is not some mysterious prefiguration, in a minor historical event, of a major religious apocalypse, but only the more ragged sense that what happens in a well forgotten episode of mob violence is not *so* different from the Event which everyone has agreed to remember. Evidently Hawthorne's interest in "The Matter of the Revolution" was not limited to the terms of Puritan typology. What this suggests, further, is that Hawthorne's reading in colonial history may have been more purposive than is sometimes assumed.[13]

Especially instructive, in this regard, are the terms of the unresolved critical debate on the "Molineux" problem. A rare case in the annals of Hawthorne criticism, the tale was given its first professional sponsorship by "historicists," powerfully persuaded that Hawthorne's account of the violent expulsion of a Tory leader was meant to prefigure the loss and gain—or the imputed guilt—of America's separation from England. Psychoanalytic readers protested, almost at once, that the true interest in the story is the *personal* one, of Robin's ambivalent search for some indulgent paternal influence, and that the "revolutionary" violence which engulfs him is itself best understood as a resistance to "the father"; thus all historical readings unduly particularize the tale. Yet the discovery of names and faces and issues sharply relevant to America's provincial circumstances has caused the particularist reading to remain strong, encouraging a sort of polite compromise: In this story, perhaps, political revolution and oedipal overthrow simply figure one another, endlessly, without subordination or primacy of interest.[14]

On this supple premise, the American Revolution comes to seem just like the act or process of growing up—painful and even violent, as the overthrow of paternal authority must always be, whether literal or figurative; yet not less inevitable for that reason, as nations, just like young men, must surely assume their own "separate and equal station." Still, the scrupulous reader may observe that this conciliatory view quietly elides the one consideration the tale tries hardest to problematize: the intriguing but not always attractive question of "conspiracy."

Quite obviously, most of the story's broad humor and all its irony about "shrewdness" depend on the fact that Robin is the only character in the story who does not know what the local politicos have in store for his kinsman, that very evening. Robin has stumbled into something, well over his head, and its planned events take place in total disregard for his own psychic case. He is forced to grow up, we might say, *just when* some other men are plotting the ouster of an obnoxious local authority, but the logic of the two events is separate enough. It may flatter some theorists to observe that he does, momentarily at least, join in with the general will to revolt. But plots and cabals are entirely alien to his countrified adolescence. And—as it would be naive to suppose that a tar-and-feather procession has come about in a purely natural "course of human events"—we are left with an important reminder: Revolutions are plotted in a way that maturation never is. To imply that the one is as natural and inevitable as the other is to obscure the question of political responsibility.[15]

Some of the tale's best ironies touch just this question of conspiratorial difference. At a moment of potential clarification, Robin asks the stranger who joins him at the meetinghouse if he "'happen[s] to know'" the fellow with the face painted half-red and half-black. "'Not intimately,'" comes the reply, "'but I chanced to meet him a little time previous ... [and] you may trust his word ... that the Major will very shortly pass through this street'" (82). Obviously the stranger *knows*. And surely his answer is as ironical as Robin's question is innocent: Needing to be in just the right place at just the right time, he has met with the man (of a lower social order) delegated to head the parade which he and other, more powerful but less conspicuous leaders have carefully arranged. Evidently nothing like "chance" was in any way involved. Clearly it is only Robin himself who just happens to be there, where the Molineux procession is duly scheduled to pass in review.

Not coincidentally, perhaps, the same sort of irony is playing about the tale's curious headnote. After rehearsing some arcane materials from the "annals of Massachusetts," an obviously learned narrator seems suddenly anxious to spare us a "long and dry detail of colonial affairs"; but when his forgiving formula suggests that "the following adventures ... *chanced* upon a summer night, not far from a hundred years ago" (68, my italics), we recognize a first version of the forget-real-politics fallacy the tale itself exists to identify and undo. For only in pure romance would all this ritual activity just "happen" to provide the context for an aspiring hero's *rite de passage*. The American Revolution was nothing such. And not even Shakespeare's "Dream" reads this way any more.

Most readers can appreciate the pace and the pathos of Robin's "evening of ambiguity and weariness" (80) without knowing the cause and extent of the rum riots of the 1730s. They may even get along without recalling that a certain kind of nepotistic politics had once acquired the name of a "Robinocracy." But the story of American political resistance in the eighteenth century is no longer credible without reference to the mob actions that were thoroughly stage-managed by the respectable leaders of colonial society.[16] And what is most noteworthy about Robin's psychic adventure is that absolutely nothing in his growing resistance to figures of paternal authority has quite prepared him for this encounter with the politics of "controlled" and "ritual" violence. Adrift in the city, balked at every turn, cudgel in hand, ready to club anyone you please, Robin may seem ripe for a wider rebellion. But his enduring naivete—a type of our own apolitical criticism, perhaps—has no way of coping with the art of overthrow; evidently some other, more circumstantial initiation is yet to be faced.[17]

Yet the logic of "Roger Malvin's Burial" may offer an even more severe education in the competing claims of general principle and historical circumstance. It is, on one hand, the tale most boldly claimed by the psychoanalytic science of Frederick Crews; and indeed the experience of its protagonist seems compulsed and nightmarish even after Crews has recanted his systematic Freudianism.[18] On the other hand, however, it attaches itself to an event far more obscure than the American Revolution or even the Salem Witchcraft. For—apart from the tale's own headnote—what modern reader has even *heard* of "Lovell's Fight"?

Innocent of all such concerns, Crews opposed instead certain orthodox approaches to the case of Reuben Bourne: Unless one were extremely wary about the ending of this disturbing tale, one had better not venture a religious interpretation at all. What happens there is more barbarous than pious or at any rate, more psychologically elemental than rationally moral. Reuben Bourne may feel that "his sin was expiated" (107) in the killing of his son, but (unless one posits a "teleological suspension of the ethical")[19] the issue is not salvation but psychic survival. The plot of which is clear enough: Ineffectually remorseful ever since his abandonment of his prospective father-in-law, Reuben has thwarted himself in business, poisoned his social relations, then wandered compulsively back to the spot where it all began, to expiate in slaughter what began in grief. Obscurely guilty of the death of a figurative father, he frees his tormented soul by killing—not *quite* accidentally—his literal son. "Regeneration Through Violence"[20] with a vengeance.

Chastened, the moralist may protest that it requires less than oedipal theory to notice that Reuben will suffer great distress at the decision he seems forced to make: Heroically, he would like to remain beside his dying companion in arms; as a Christian, perhaps, he would like to "lay down his life for his friend"; yet he is utilitarian enough to realize the greatest good of the greatest number; and he would like to save his own skin. He sees at once the truth of Malvin's prediction: Dorcas will be upset at first, but she will come around; things will be awkward in the meantime, but they must be endured. Yet it is this very meantime that Reuben fears he cannot endure: He knows that Dorcas's eyes, if not her voice, will accuse him of cowardice; and he cannot face this refracted version of himself. This is why he allows a tough and ruefully smiling Malvin to persuade him that his real project is to go off and seek a means of rescue. Only thus can he save his life and still maintain the standard of heroism objectified in the glance of Dorcas.

Clearly, this old-fashioned psychology is as relevant as Freud. Source critics might even observe that Reuben's moral dilemma is constructed as a traditional "case of conscience," the very sort of problem treated in one of Hawthorne's favorite seventeenth-century authors.[21] Indeed this older style of motive analysis—pressing rational analysis to the point of disappearance—may even explain why Reuben feels guilty in the first place: not for refusing "the gratuitous sacrifice of his own life," but for "concealment" (98), of both fact and motive, from all concerned. Including himself.

What draws Reuben back, compulsively, to the spot where he left Malvin is the memory of his unreedemed vow. Baffled by his options, Reuben had promised to return, if not to rescue Malvin, then at least to bury him. Yet this becomes impossible the moment he is less than honest with Dorcas: She inquires for her father and, as he rambles on about the terrible complexity of his forest scene, she falsely infers that her father died with Reuben nearby and was buried by him. Reuben merely holds back the truth; yet when she spreads the tale of his wonderful "courage and fidelity" (97), he is trapped in his own deceptive silence. Nor is this "mental reservation" unrelated to his original mixture of motive. The situation turns out exactly as he had imagined: She expects heroism and he cannot bear to confess ordinariness; he lets her conclude exactly what he, looking at himself through her eyes, had himself wished to believe. And the whole problem had arisen, some old-time casuist might observe, because Reuben has failed to be clear about his real intentions, to "settle his own motives."

Yet the possible application of moral categories is not at all the main problem with the psychological approach to this tale. The more crucial question, surely, is where either of these analyses leaves the reader who happens to wonder what any of this could have to do with an incident of "Indian warfare" (88). Generalists may prefer to see the tale's headnote as written under a kind of polite erasure. Yet one could also read it as a picque to historical curiosity; and surely no one can *forbid* an inquiry into the possible relevance of "Lovell's Fight."

Source hunters long ago traced a number of the story's symbolic details—Reuben's bloody handkerchief, most famously—to various accounts of what transpired when Lovewell's raiders went out to meet the Natives on a mission of protective retaliation. More recently, a truly inspired sleuth finally discovered the obvious: The oak tree to which Reuben ties that handkerchief looks exactly like the Charter Oak from the flag of Connecticut, held sacred by colonials ever since they hid, in the original, the land titles they meant to protect from the King of England.[22] Evidently the question of bloody wars for territory is supposed to occur to somebody, not utterly distracted by the strife or the delicacy of Reuben's after-the-fact dilemma. For it is after one of the most curious facts in the entire provincial period of New England.

We can—if we think about "The Matter of the Indians" at all— easily imagine that "Lovell's Fight" was probably not a very grand affair, whatever "its consequences to the country"; no doubt its historian can achieve "romance" only by "casting certain circumstances judiciously into the shade" (88). Indeed, Lovewell's men were bounty hunters, seeking Indians at the astonishing value of one hundred pounds per scalp; among other ventures, none very glorious to either side, they managed to kill a small party of Indians while they slept, then got themselves ambushed in pursuit of a single Indian who appeared unarmed but who may have been a decoy. Many of their number were killed outright; some stragglers died in the attempt to return to the settlements; a few escaped to tell the tale.[23] By which tale hangs Hawthorne's own, though this plot might require a little cynicism to predict.

Evidently the first returning witness misrepresented certain circumstances of the expedition—not to his fiancee (though in fact he had been scalping Indians for money to get married), but to his minister who, not unlike the Dorcas of our tale, immediately turned the affair into a ballad of chivalry. His story took hold and was widely republished and rewritten, even after many in Lovewell's town had come to know the less heroic version. With the result that, a hundred years later, just as Hawthorne was graduating from college and preparing to enter the solemn career of making an original American literature out of authentic American materials, a whole culture was preparing to celebrate the centenary of that famous "Fight." One of Hawthorne's professors produced a hymn for the occasion; so did his classmate Longfellow. A Salem newspaper even ran a front-page story on just how and when to hold the celebration.[24] Historical science having recovered the exact date, a pious and grateful people might recall the deeds by which their ancestors had secured the land they now occupied. And—in the midst of a national policy of "Indian Removal"—they would renew their "covenantal" dedication to the same historic values.

The ironies are mostly self-evident. One need not romanticize the Indians to notice that a local embarrassment had been turned into a National Cultural Treasure. People made pilgrimages to a monument erected near "Lovewell's Pond." For the moment, at least, "Lovewell's Rock" was better known than the one filiopietism had tried to drag from the seacoast to the center of Plymouth. And both these monuments—with many others, in fact and literature—expressed the same sense as the famous one at Bunker Hill, the elective destiny of America. Given these circumstances, might one not expect a writer who once suggested building a monument to the supposed witches on the Gallows Hill of Salem Village[25] to mark the occasion in some unorthodox way? And how better than with the story of a would-be hero who spoils life and prevents posterity with an historical lie about the ragged facts of the sad provincial case? For Reuben indeed operates as an historian; and Dorcas too, after she has functioned first as his imagined and then his literal audience. Together they fashion a tale in which, though there is undeniable tragedy, yet everyone acts as nobly as possible and all things turn out for the best. And yet there is, well advertised in the headnote to their fateful little romance, the memory of "certain circumstances" which the interest of history had better not repress. True, it requires a certain determined provincialism to read the tale this way; but the alternative may be just as unsettling. For it may be a good deal easier to rehearse the structure of the psyche than to recover the unlovely actualities of the colonial past. And, as we have yet to suggest, even Hawthorne's Puritan tales may look to circumstances as much as to the soul.

3

The outline of "Young Goodman Brown" is quite simple; but the account it provides seems almost too compressed. A noticeably unsuspecting young man spends a single night in a suspicious-looking forest and returns to spend the rest of an unhappy life suspecting everyone. At one moment this still-resisting protagonist is loudly proclaiming that he "will yet stand firm" (282); but then, in the fluttering of a few pink ribbons, his "Faith is gone." By which he means, shockingly, that "There is no good on earth; and sin is but a name" (283). He may as well give *himself* over to the Devil. It all happens so fast: we seem to have missed something. What power in the world could have utterly overset the painful teaching and sober practice of a whole pious lifetime—transforming a moment of moral panic into a studied and lethal blasphemy? And with such violence?

The narrator suggests, as Brown goes tearing into "the heart of the dark wilderness," that he is simply following "the instinct that guides mortal man to evil" (283). Yet this "Calvinistic" law can account for the direction but not the pace or the timing of Brown's sudden moral collapse: Why had he not been following that path all along? Nor can it quite explain the overdetermination of his new-found despair: Is nihilism the proper opposite of "faith"? Nor does it at all predict the fact that Brown will try to pull himself back from the precipice toward which he is rushing: is it an *evil* instinct which prompts him to cry out to Faith, at the lurid climax of the witch meeting, "Look up to Heaven, and resist the Wicked One!" (288)? Evidently something more is at stake than Melville's suspicion of "innate depravity and original sin."[26]

Something altogether more primal, the psychoanalytic reader is sure to suggest: Brown's readiness to overthrow all authority is instantaneous because it is a given of adolescent experience. And if Brown is a little old for this onset of oedipal hostility, that fact may well account for the rage in his response. His "manhood" has been pent up and smoldering too long; not wisely socialized but too well inhibited by fathers and ministers and even a prim little wife, it will not go forever without finding its moment of eruption. The story merely gives us that moment. As Brown's Devil is nothing more than the emergence of his most unpuritanical unconscious, so the witch meeting in the forest is pure fantasy—for Brown as surely as for his creator. It is not insistently sexual for nothing. And no one should be surprised if Hawthorne chooses the moralistic world of latter-day Puritanism to stand for the problem Freud called "Civilization and its Discontents."[27]

"Be it so, if you will" (288), as the narrator says in response to his own proposed reduction of Brown's twilight-zone experience: There is no reason to suppose Hawthorne believed in the Devil any more literally than do we ourselves; nor need we resist according him a certain prescience about the silent power of sexuality in controlling our motives and centering our identity. Yet Hawthorne's Puritan sources were very much concerned with the question of diabolical agency, and perhaps this provides some other clue to the violence and speed of Brown's rebellious outburst.

It may be only a rare historical joke that the tale evokes Brown's visit to the forest in one of Puritanism's most famous self-descriptions— an "errand" (276) into the "wilderness" (283),[28] but elsewhere the language is as apt as it is official. What it insists is that, however we describe the Devil that erupts from Goodman Brown at the moment of his "horrid blasphemy" (284), another Devil has been conjured well in advance; and that, for all our sense that Brown gets more than he has bargained for, there has indeed been a bargain. From which Goodman Brown tries, at first, to back out: "'Friend.... having kept covenant by meeting thee here, it is my purpose now to return whence I came'" (278).

Brown could hardly have used a more telling and technical word to describe his agreement with the figure who leads him along the forest path. In his world, "covenant" named not only the pact the Calvinist God had made with Christ, by which his obedient sacrifice came to count as reparation for the sins of mankind, but also the agreement by which the saints accepted this vicarious atonement. It served, further, as a mystic substitute for terms like contract or compact in the Puritan's consensual theory of government. And most pointedly, it named the origin and essence of the particular church or congregation. Other churches might claim to exist on some a priori or "catholic" basis, but Puritan churches came into being only when self-professing saints enacted a covenant, among themselves and with God, to walk in His ways. Thus, as historians of witchcraft have pointed out, it could serve to name that unspeakable agreement by which reprobates might swear to walk, antithetically, in the ways of His Archenemy.[29] Well may Goodman Brown hope *this* covenant is not yet sealed.

The fact that Brown manages to avoid parodic baptism *in nomine diaboli* suggests that it is not. And indeed the initial intention of his "errand" seems more tentative than simply to "go over." In the more easily supposable case, someone still failing, after a long and anxious time, to discover any trustworthy signs of election by God might grow desperate; in this mood he might get word that, though God's was surely the only covenant *in town*, there was another, inverted one, off in the forest. The reader of *The Scarlet Letter* will recall that Mistress Hibbins appeals to a despairing Hester Prynne in just such terms; and though Hester resists, the appeal might be very strong indeed, Orthodoxy stoutly held that whole lives might have to be lived out with no assurance beyond that of hope itself, but imagination inferred that here and there some "Ishmael" might despair of ever being recognized as one of God's adopted—declaring, in the formula Emerson made bold to appropriate, "If I am the Devil's child, I will live then from the Devil"; and most suitably, perhaps, if that tortured "I" could share the misery Dickinson called that "white sustenance, despair." A terrible prospect, yet perhaps "a guilty identity ... was better than none."[30]

But the story of Goodman Brown is a turn more subtle. Setting out for the forest, Brown feels guilty enough about his purposes, yet feels confident that he can make his little visit with impunity: After this one short venture into the Devil's territory, he can safely come back to town, to Faith, to everything as it was. His experiment appears to prove this impossible, but it also suggests, to him at least, that his sense of salvation may have been an illusion all along. And it is this "discovery" which turns his curiosity about the Invisible World into an express confession of diabolical loyalty. Which he then tries to take back.

Brown's wife—Faith, "aptly named," but not yet an allegory we can quite construe—entreats him to "tarry" with her on this "of all nights in the year"; perhaps it is October 31, when evil influences were known to be abroad. But he converts concern into suspicion: "'dost thou doubt me already, and we but three months married!'" And this curious mood of moral dis-ease continues. His heart smites him, understandably, for leaving his wife "on such an errand!" He even wonders whether "a dream had warned her what work is to be done to-night." But as there is no evidence of this, we infer that Brown's guilt is nervously imagining things. Then, the moment after this recognizable attack of guilty projection,[31] Brown goes on to settle his conscience and compose our allegory: "Well, she's a blessed angel on earth; and after this one night, I'll cling to her skirts and follow her to heaven" (276).

There is a question of gender here, of course, as Brown imagines his wife as a different sort of moral being. But—as it is "with this excellent resolve for the future [that] Goodman Brown felt himself justified in making more haste on his present evil purpose" (276)—there is also the problem theologians have called "presumption," the act of declaring one's salvation already certain, whatever might, occur in the rest of one's mortal life. Earlier theorists called it an "unpardonable sin," not because it was the most heinous act or thought they could imagine, but because it made nonsense out of their notion of life, all of it, as a period of testing, during which one might, at any moment, turn one's mind toward or away from the will of God.[32] And not surprisingly, Calvinist thinkers kept having to explain that their idea of eternal predestination, based not on merit, but bestowed as the gift of faith, was not just the latest invitation to this familiar moral evasion. Feeling "justified"—the technical word for one's gratuitous acceptance by God—was scarcely an excuse for laxity or experimentation. For one thing, individual assurance could never be perfect; and for another, it needed to be read from the quality of one's ethical dispositions.[33]

Certainly, therefore, the Calvinists did not intend a moral holiday. Yet they may have opened a crack in the wall of perfect behavior. And Goodman Brown appears to be creeping out at that crack, suspending the ordinary rules for a brief period, but trusting in his safety after all; assuming salvation, it appears, in spite of his devilish transgression. "Presuming on Faith," the conscience of official Puritanism might angrily declare; and invalidating the mystical "Marriage" into the bargain. "I told you so," the older system might smugly observe, and deepen its sense of triumph when Goodman Brown goes on to "despair," the only *other* unpardonable sin; the other way, that is, of nullifying the moral life at a stroke.

Yet Brown's despair is scarcely the normative case. Typically, an individual became aware of sins too great to be forgiven by God himself; this looked like an extreme of humility, but was really a bizarre form of pride, as its anatomists never tired of pointing out. Or else, as we have suggested, a Puritan might simply crack under the strain and accept the worst-case scenario. But Brown's problem is not at all a matter of such gloomy introspection; rather, with the help of his Devil, he comes to suspect the settled appearance of virtue in all his most familiar acquaintances. Then, undone by this challenge to the assumptions of his whole life, he despairs of the possibility of goodness in the world. And so fast that his logic—and our explanation—must be embedded in the terms of Puritan history.

Most simply, perhaps, in the doctrine of "visible sanctity." No fool and no mad zealot, the Puritan knew there were "hypocrites" in the churches of New England. These churches had as their explicit aim to be the purest the world had seen since the Savior had elected His own handpicked disciples. Even He had got one "Judas," and so even the most careful of men in these latter days could hardly fail to make mistakes. But members of Puritan churches who were not Saints—who dissembled or who were simply mistaken about their call from God— were to be the exception. Formally so, since by rule one had to give a public account of this call in order to be taken into "communing" membership. Elsewhere, churches might exist to *produce* saints, little by little; but in the New World Order, churches existed to identify, with all human precision, those whom God *called* to be saints, and to bring them together, visibly, into an exemplary order of holy community.[34]

Trained by their system to recognize one another, the Saints came to rely on one another for support of all kinds. Particularly, perhaps, for mutual sanction: One could *hardly* be sure of one's own election, all by oneself, particularly when the evidences of faith were so much more subtle than the older standard of behavior; then too, if one thought about it, there was the whole Anglo-Catholic world one had left behind, scorning the Calvinist theology of total depravity and irresistible grace as an insult to moral sense, and spurning as utopian the doctrine of visible sanctity. But if the whole group held together in these beliefs, the faith of all might stand. Forswearing the intermediation of priest and sacrament, the Puritan might yet find himself comparing notes: our *nature* is evil, as witness our former lives, but has not God's *grace* introduced a principle of goodness? Truly so? In my *own* case? Well, other people might recognize the grace shining forth from one's halting profession more surely than oneself, and *their* conviction—necessary to admit the would-be saint to the bosom of Faith in any event—might become the surest basis of one's own.

What this interdependency implies is the irreducibly social dimension of Puritan faith, even in so private a fact as one's election.[35] For what if an unhappy Puritan found occasion to doubt the good faith of those very individuals whose assurance of salvation had become so entwined with his own? Honestly explored, these doubts might go straight to the source of his own assurance. Even less radically applied, however, they would amount to a suspicion that the covenanting procedures of the particular church had been an empty formality, unable to discover any appreciable difference between the persons one "had met at the communion table" and those seen "rioting at the tavern" (283). Would this experience not threaten all one believed? Might it not bring on, with only some hyperbole, the nihilistic rejection of everything?

So it turns out for Goodman Brown. And so his particular Devil seems to have foreknown, as the climax of his commencement address only confirms the sense of Brown's mid-forest outburst: Evil is indeed "'the nature of mankind,'" as Calvin's theory of depravity has prepared you to discover; and now, as there is no such thing as regenerating grace, "'Evil must be your only happiness.'" But the Devil's word to the initiates has another note as well. His welcome to the Community of Evil is, before all else, a farewell to the covenantal delusion:

" 'Depending on one another's hearts, ye had hoped, that virtue were not all a dream. Now are ye undeceived!' " (287). And—among all the losses of faith that are possible—this "congregational" circumstance contributes powerfully to making Brown's loss a particularly memorable instance.

Equally important, however, is the logic which effects that undeception. We follow well enough the steps by which Brown comes to feel that he and Faith are "the only pair ... yet hesitating on the verge of wickedness" (287). If all these trusted and familiar Saints turn out to be the Devil's own, then so must the rest of this wretched world as well. But what *of* those supposed Saints? Has Goodman Brown been reliably informed about their true allegiance? Are they indeed all in league with the Prince of Darkness? Or is there reason to suppose that Brown has been deceived? Could there be something wrong with his evidence, even where plain sight has supplied an ocular proof?

We might begin by recalling that not all that evidence has been visible. The process begins, in fact, with hearsay, a couple of stories about the misdeeds of Brown's ancestors; and though it moves on from there, to the sight of the irreverent Goody Cloyse and the lascivious church officers, there seems no marked change of mood or conviction. The Devil is prosecuting his proper case, and Brown's responses are perfectly continuous: sad business, but no rule for the likes of a "simple husbandman" (279) like me; and besides, there's always "My Faith." Then come the pink ribbons, and it's all over but the blasphemous shouting. Yet not even these most material objects can quite disturb the reader's sense of a single shape and direction—a single epistemology— of the whole sequence. If there is a climax, it involves the ordering of the persons charged rather than the evidence presented. It is as if the line between imagination and being, perception and conviction, suspicion and proof had entirely disappeared; as if one had merely to lead Brown's attention from one fantastic projection to another.

Certainly this impression will be strongest in the reader who notices that none of the characters Brown meets on the forest path seems to cast a shadow, and that they appear and disappear in the most remarkably convenient manner, as if conjured by the Companion's "snakelike staff" (279). Curiosity about this magical quality ought to be enhanced by the observation that each of these exemplary apparitions is referred to as a "figure" or a "shape," as if to reserve judgment on their proper mode of existence. And it is precisely in this mood that a reader may profit to discover—in a learned article by David Levin—the antique doctrine of "specters," those mysterious simulacra of physical appearance which made it possible for persons to appear in places remote from their locus of true and substantial being. And to learn, too, of the controversy, in Brown's own (third-generation) New England, about the Devil's power to manipulate these spectral appearances.[36]

Most authorities taught that the Devil regularly did assume the shape of his sworn disciples—whenever he went abroad to carry out their guilty wishes. And this understanding made it possible for the witch accusers to maintain their allegations against persons who could otherwise account for their whereabouts: I must have seen their *specters*. The crisis arose when someone thought to ask whether the Devil had the power to assume the shape of a person who had *not* freely chosen his covenant, to cause a Saint to appear in the most compromising of places and postures. The magistrates appointed to conduct the proceedings against the accused witches thought a just God would never permit the exercise of a power so fatal to the cause of human faith. But a panel of experts returned the opinion that the Devil might well enjoy that very power: What else could Scripture mean by declaring that "the Devil has appeared as an Angel of Light"?

The story of the events which followed the proclamation of this unsettling possibility has held a terrible fascination for those who have pursued the historical record—including Arthur Miller, whose dramatic rendition (in *The Crucible*) has caused the metaphor of "witch hunt" to stand for all sorts of accusations which admit no refutation. Here, however, there are no courtroom recriminations; and no hint of that general breakdown of faith Hawthorne elsewhere refers to as a "Universal Madness riot in the Main-street" (1047). Only the possibility that Brown may be witnessing not the real activities of his fellow congregationalists but only the meretricious antics of their spectral shapes. We cannot be sure.[37]

In his running contest with the Devil, Goodman Brown has tried to make it all depend on his "Faith"; and so in the end it does, though in a way his presumptuous confidence had little prepared him to expect. Did Faith indeed "look up to heaven and resist the Wicked One"? Was she in fact even there? or was it her specter, stolen by the Devil for the express purpose of tempting the faith of Goodman Brown? He never can know. She may well be as innocent as Shakespeare's Desdemona—whose innocence, as a modern reading has observed, can never be known by Othello in the same way that *she herself* knows it.[38] Nor can the story itself inform us without entirely compromising its own epistemology: We never do know the intentions of others, not as they themselves know them. As intentional reality is hidden, so all moral appearances are in an important sense spectral: We observe the shape but do not behold the substance. Best to reserve judgment, therefore, ascribing to others, always, the same degree of good faith we habitually discern in ourselves; best to assume that others' resistance to Evil is about equal to our own.

Doubt, in this sense, becomes the source of, even participates in, the nature of faith: The negative term signifies only our unhappiness about the fact that we cannot know certain things for sure; the positive one, our recognition that we have nevertheless to make up our minds and act. All Goodman Brown can know, in the end, is that, after keeping his initial covenant, he recoiled from the Devil's baptism; he flirted with the power of Evil, so to speak, but did not in the end espouse it. Might he not suppose that the wishes of his wife have been equally hypothetical? Failing this sort of ascriptive trust, his final gloom reveals nothing so plainly as the lasting effect of his initial bad faith: The guilty self-knowledge which caused him to suspect Faith of suspecting him assumes its settled form in doubting the victory of her virtue. The problem has its "psychoanalytic" side, of course, but it requires less than a full course of "analysis." For if Brown's bad faith puts forth, from the beginning, the textbook traits of "guilty projection," the same must be said of Spenser's Red Cross Knight, whose deception by the "dreamy" machinations of Archimago had long since suggested that "specter evidence is but a curious name for the shameless tendency to discover in others, as fact, the guilty wish we repress in ourselves."[39] And more important, in any case, may be Hawthorne's historical re-application of this Spenserian principle—to a set of theological circumstances that matter as much as the more political ones in "Molineux" and "Malvin."

Not that Hawthorne has solved the question of "What Happened in Salem." It is worth noting that, where his contemporaries tried to rationalize the problem of witchcraft—by invoking the quasi-medical notion of "hysteria," or by appealing to the pseudohistorical idea of "superstition"—Hawthorne is careful to let this limit phenomenon retain something of its terrible wonder.[40] We learn to suspect that people who discover witches are telling us more about themselves than about the persons they accuse; but "Young Goodman Brown" has nothing to say about what persons did and did not indulge this self-betraying behavior.

What this taut little tale observes, instead, is that the discovery of Saints and the detection of witches were parts of the same problem, that specter evidence was simply the negative test case of visible sanctity. In morally opposite but epistemologically identical instances, certain official persons needed to make reliable judgments about the soul *in extremis*. Beyond actions, which are various; beyond even intentions, which may be fleeting and even whimsical; the Puritan had to identify the deep spiritual orientation of another person. Here is a soul, solemnly requesting admission to the sacrament which sets the seal on the mystery of salvation: is it sworn to God, finally, beyond all possibility of change or mistake? Or, as the curiously unfolding historical plot suddenly reversed itself, has it perhaps made that other oath? Sooner or later, in the latter, parodic instance if not in the former, normative one, this dedicated group of religionists would surely discover that their most important judgments were all more or less projective. Needing to know what cannot certainly be known—the true spiritual estate of another person—such judges must put in the place where literal "in-sight" is denied a hypothetical version of their own relevant experience.

In the matter of Puritan church admissions, the official insistence that everyone exercise the "judgment of charity" came close to recognizing the peril: judge the faith of others, always, by the light of one's own best faith. But then, by a reversal of logic and a lapse of sympathy one notes without quite understanding, the witchcraft proceedings of 1692 seemed to invert their own rule: Saints are known by faith but witches by suspicion. Indeed, Brown's swift progress—from believing in those who have believed in him, to doubting all virtue but his own—seems invented to mimic the outline of this definitive Puritan dilemma. And though we can learn to state this problem in some remarkably general ways, the story itself seems remarkably loyal to its very own circumstances. By its logic, the history of the lapsed Faith of Puritanism remains a capital way of learning the benefit of doubt.

NOTES

1. The assumptions I ascribe to "most readers" would find support in at least two important modern schools of critical opinion: in the so-called "New Criticism," which insists that literary meaning is entirely "internal" to the text; and also (more recently) in the variety of "Reader Response" theories, which stress the extent to which literary meaning is a production of the individual reader. For a brief exposition of these positions, see M. H. Abrams, *A Glossary of Literary Terms* (New York: Holt, Rinehart, and Winston, 1985), pp. 223–4, 231–4. For more extensive discussion of the theory of internalism, see Murray Krieger, *The New Apologists for Poetry* (Minneapolis: University of Minnesota Press, 1956); *Theory of Criticism* (Baltimore: Johns Hopkins University Press, 1976); and Vincent B. Leitch, *American Literary Criticism* (New York: Columbia University Press, 1988), pp. 24–59. And for a sample of the theories that empower the reader, see Jane P. Tompkins, ed., *Reader-Response Criticism* (Baltimore: Johns Hopkins University Press, 1980).

2. For professional complaint about the unpreparedness of the American student, see Allan Bloom, *The Closing of the American Mind* (New York: Simon and Schuster, 1987); and E. D. Hirsch, *Cultural Literacy* (Boston: Houghton Mifflin, 1987).

3. For a brief introduction to the incipient theory and practice of the "New Historicism," see Ross C. Murfin, "What is the New Historicism?" in Murfin, ed., *The Scarlet Letter* (Boston: St. Martin's Press, 1991), pp. 333–44. For fuller treatments, see H. Aram Veeser, ed., *The New Historicism* (New York: Routledge, 1989); and Brook Thomas, *The New Historicism* (Princeton, N.J.: Princeton University Press, 1991).

4. For an epitome of the achievement of Hawthorne "source studies," see Neal Frank Doubleday, *Hawthorne's Early Tales* (Durham, N.C.: Duke University Press, 1972).

5. In context, Hawthorne's remark about "burrowing ... into the depths of our common nature, for the purposes of psychological romance" reads not as a rejection of history but as a defense against "egotism"; see Hawthorne's Preface to *The Snow-image*, in *Hawthorne: Tales and Sketches* (New York: Library of America, 1982), p. 1154.

6. See, for example, Frederick Crews, *The Sins of the Fathers* (New York: Oxford University Press, 1966), especially chap. 2, "The Sense of the Past," pp. 27–43.

7. For Emerson's most famous defense of the proposition that "There is one mind common to all individual men," see "History," in *The Collected Works of Ralph Waldo Emerson*, vol. 2, Alfred R. Ferguson and Jean Ferguson Carr, eds. (Cambridge: Harvard University Press, 1979), pp. 3–23. This essay compresses the argument of his lecture series on "The Philosophy of History"; see *The Early Lectures of Ralph Waldo Emerson*, vol. 2, Stephen E. Whicher, Robert E. Spiller, and Wallace E. Williams, eds. (Cambridge: Harvard University Press, 1964), pp. 1–188.

8. The story of Hawthorne's early career as a writer of tales involves his serious but failed attempts to publish collections of tales which might answer the widespread complaint that America was not a "storied" nation: "Seven Tales of My Native Land," ca. 1825–27; "Provincial Tales," ca. 1828–29; and "The Story Teller," 1831–34. For discussion, see Nelson F. Adkins, "The Early Projected Works of Nathaniel Hawthorne," *Papers of the Bibliographical Society of America* 39 (1945), 119–55; Nina Baym, *The Shape of Hawthorne's Career* (Ithaca: Cornell University Press, 1976), pp. 15-52; and Michael J. Colacurcio, Introduction to *Nathaniel Hawthorne: Selected Tales and Sketches* (New York: Penguin, 1987), esp. pp. vii–xxv.

9. The other early "witchcraft" tales are "The Hollow of the Three Hills" (1830), originally intended for "Seven Tales," and "Alice Doane's Appeal" (1835), apparently a reworking of an earlier "Alice Doane," probably intended for that same volume. For "The Matter of Puritanism" as but one subject of importance to the interest of an American literature, see Rufus Choate's 1833 Salem lecture on "The Importance of Illustrating New England History by a Series of Romances Like the Waverley Novels," in *Works* (Boston: Little, Brown, 1862), vol. 1, pp. 319–46. For discussion, see Doubleday, *Early Tales*, pp. 24–6.

10. For the significance of the dating of "The Minister's Black Veil," see Michael J. Colacurcio, *The Province of Piety* (Cambridge: Harvard University Press, 1984), pp. 312–85.

11. All citations of the text of Hawthorne's tales, given in parentheses, are from *Hawthorne: Tales and Sketches* (New York: Library of America, 1982).

12. For the English background of the "The May-Pole of Merry Mount," see Doubleday, *Early Tales*, pp. 97–9; and J. Gary Williams,

"History in Hawthorne's 'May-Pole of Merry Mount,'" *Essex Institute Historical Collections* 108 (1972), 3–30.

13. In an 1837 letter to former classmate Longfellow, Hawthorne admits he has "turned over a good many books," but only, he protests, "in so desultory a way that it cannot be called study"; see *Nathaniel Hawthorne: The Letters, 1813–1843*, Thomas Woodson, L. Neal Smith, and Norman Holmes Pearson, eds. (Columbus: The Ohio State University Press, 1984), p. 252. For discussion, see Colacurcio, *Province*, pp. 71–8.

14. For the historicist view of "My Kinsman, Major Molineux" (MKMM), see Q. D. Leavis, "Hawthorne as Poet," *Sewanee Review* 50 (1951), 198–205; and Roy Harvey Pearce, "Hawthorne and the Sense of the Past," *ELH* 21 (1954), 327–34. For the psychological response, see Hyatt H. Waggoner, *Hawthorne* (Cambridge: Harvard University Press, 1955), pp. 46–53; and Seymour Gross, "Hawthorne's MKMM: History as Moral Adventure," *Nineteenth-Century Fiction* 12 (1957), 97–109. For the attempt at reconciliation, see Robert H. Fossum, *Hawthorne's Inviolable Circle* (Deland: FL: Everett/Edwards, 1972), pp. 26–31; and Peter Shaw, "Fathers, Sons, and the Ambiguities of Revolution in MKMM," *New England Quarterly* 49 (1976), 559–76.

15. For Jefferson's attempt to "naturalize" the coming of the American Revolution, see Garry Wills, *Inventing America* (Garden City, NY: Doubleday, 1978), pp. 93–110. For an account of Americans' self-forgiving view of their "Coming of Age," see Michael Kammen, *A Season of Youth* (New York: Knopf, 1978), pp. 186–220.

16. On the question of "Robinocracy," see James Duban, "Robins and Robinarchs in MKMM," *Nineteenth-Century Fiction* 38 (1983), 27–188. For the management of mobs in eighteenth-century America, see Arthur M. Schlesinger, "Political Mobs and the American Revolution," *Massachusetts Historical Society Proceedings* 99 (1955), esp. pp. 244–50; Edmund S. and Helen M. Morgan, *The Stamp Act Crisis* (Chapel Hill: University of North Carolina Press, 1953), pp. 159–68, 231–40; G. B. Warden, *Boston 1689–1776* (Boston: Little Brown, 1970), pp. 92–101; Gary B. Nash, *Urban Crucible* (Cambridge: Harvard University Press, 1979), pp. 292–311; and Peter Shaw, *American Patriots and the Rituals of Revolution* (Cambridge: Harvard University Press, 1981), pp. 5–47. For application of these matters to MKMM, see Shaw, "Hawthorne's Ritual Typology of the American Revolution," *Prospects* 3 (1977), 483–98; and Colacurcio, *Province*, pp. 130–53 (bibliography, pp. 562–71).

17. For readings which resist the conclusion that Robin has learned his needful lessons—"or will have when apprehension becomes knowledge" (Gross, "Moral Adventure," p. 108)—see John P. McWilliams, Jr., *Hawthorne, Melville and the American Character* (Cambridge: Cambridge University Press, 1984), pp. 85–8; Frederick Newberry, *Hawthorne's Divided Loyalties* (Rutherford, NJ: Fairleigh Dickinson University Press, 1987), pp. 62–5. And for an emerging emphasis on Robin's problems of manhood in a new, urban environment, see David Leverenz, *Manhood and the American Renaissance* (Ithaca: Cornell University Press, 1989), pp. 231–9; and T. Walter Herbert, "Doing Cultural Work: MKMM and the Construction of the Self-Made Man," *Studies in the Novel* 23 (1991), 20–7.

18. For Crews's strictly Freudian reading of "Roger Malvin's Burial" (RMB), see "The Logic of Compulsion in RMB," *PMLA* 79 (1964), 457-65; and cp. *Sins*, pp. 80–95. A more distanced attitude toward Freud is expressed, *passim*, in *Out of My System* (New York: Oxford University Press, 1975); and explicitly revisionary remarks on Hawthorne are offered in *Skeptical Engagements* (New York: Oxford University Press, 1986), pp. xiii–xiv.

19. Thus Søren Kierkegaard has described the "existential" demand of Genesis 22, as a transcendent God requires Abraham (consciously) to sacrifice his son Isaac (but intervenes to provide an animal substitute). For readings which take this religious paradigm as seriously as possible, see Ely Stock, "History and Bible in Hawthorne's RMB," *Essex Institute Historical Collections* 100 (1964), 279–96; and Emily Miller Budick, *Fiction and Historical Consciousness* (New Haven: Yale University Press, 1989), pp. 36–54.

20. Richard Slotkin reads the ending of RMB as an explicit critique of frontier mythology; see *Regeneration Through Violence* (Middletown, CT: Wesleyan University Press, 1973), pp. 477–8, 483–4. On the issue of the frontier in RMB, see also Edwin Fussell, *Frontier* (Princeton: Princeton University Press, 1965), pp. 75–7; Ann Ronald, "Roger Malvin's Grandson," *Studies in American Fiction* 12 (1984), 71–7; and James McIntosh, "Nature and Frontier in RMB," *American Literature* 60 (1988), 188–204.

21. The importance to Hawthorne of the seventeenth-century "casuist" Jeremy Taylor was first established by Neal F. Doubleday, "The Theme of Hawthorne's 'Fancy's Show Box,'" *American Literature*

10 (1938), 431–3. For a full account of Taylor's influence on RMB, see Colacurcio, *Province*, pp. 109–14.

22. For the *realpolitik* of Hawthorne's "symbolic" tree, see John Samson, "Hawthorne's Oak Tree," *American Literature* 52 (1980), 457–61. Earlier source studies include G. Harrison Orians, "The Source of Hawthorne's RMB," *American Literature* 10 (1938) 313–18; David S. Lovejoy, "Lovewell's Fight and Hawthorne's RMB," *New England Quarterly* 27 (1954), 527–30; and Stock, "History and Bible." For full-scale thematic uses of these materials, see Robert J. Daly, "History and Chivalric Myth in RMB," *Essex Institute Historical Collections* 109 (1973), 99–115; and Colacurcio, *Province*, 107–30 (bibliography, pp. 556–62).

23. For the factual account of the Lovewell affair, see Fanny Hardy Eckstorm, "Pigwacket and Parson Symmes," *New England Quarterly* 9 (1936), 378–402; and Gail Bickford, "Lovewell's Fight, 1725–1958," *American Quarterly* 10 (1958), 358–66. But for a reading of RMB which insists we not romanticize the Natives—and which challenges the ironic reading of Hawthorne's headnote—see David Levin, "Modern Misjudgements of Racial Imperialism in Hawthorne and Parkman," *Yearbook of English Studies* 13 (1983), 145–58.

24. *Salem Gazette* (15 April 1825), p. 30; for analysis, see Colacurcio, *Province*, pp. 128–30.

25. Near the end of "Alice Doane's Appeal," the narrator suggests that as we "build the memorial column on the height which our fathers made sacred with their blood," so "here"—on the Gallows Hill—"should arise another monument, sadly commemorative of the errors of an earlier race, and not to be cast down, while the human heart has one infirmity which may result in crime" (*Tales*, p. 216).

26. For Melville's response to "Young Goodman Brown" (YGB), see "Hawthorne and his Mosses," conveniently reprinted in the Norton Critical Edition of *Moby-Dick*, Harrison Hayford and Hershel Parker, eds. (New York, 1967), pp. 535–51.

27. For more or less Freudian readings of YGB, see Crews, *Sins*, pp. 98–106; Reginald Cook, "The Forest of Goodman Brown's Night," *New England Quarterly* 43 (1970), 473–81; and Edward Jayne, "Pray Tarry with me Young Goodman Brown," *Literature and Psychology* 29 (1979), 100–13. For a newer style of (Lacanian) analysis, see Elizabeth Wright, "The New Psychoanalysis and Literary Criticism," *Poetics Today* 3 (1982), 89–105.

28. "Errand into the Wilderness" titles an election sermon delivered in Massachusetts in 1670 by Samuel Danforth; in after years, that much referenced sermon lent its title to one of Perry Miller's most probing inquiries into the Puritans' original motive and latter-day morale. For a brief application, see Bill Christopherson, "YGB as Historical Allegory," *Studies in Short Fiction* 23 (1986), 202–4.

29. For the full *valeur* of "covenant" in the Puritan world, see Perry Miller, *The New England Mind: The Seventeenth Century* (Cambridge: Harvard University Press, 1939), 365–462. As Miller notes elsewhere, "the heinousness of [the] crime [of witchcraft] was the fact that it, like regeneration, took the form of a covenant"; see *The New England Mind: From Colony to Province* (Cambridge: Harvard University Press, 1953). p. 193.

30. For the theology of Ishmael (and Isaac), see Thomas Werge, "*Moby-Dick* and the Calvinist Tradition," *Studies in the Novel* 1 (1969), 484–506. The Emerson quotation is from "Self-Reliance," the Dickinson from "I cannot live with you" (640). The verdict about a "guilty identity" is adapted from that of Crews on Hawthorne himself (*Sins*, p. 38).

31. For the psychology of projection in Hawthorne, see Crews, *Sins*, esp. pp. 53–60.

32. For a review of the traditional theology of presumption and despair as applied to YGB, see Joseph T. McCullen, "YGB: Presumption and Despair," *Discourse* 2 (1959), 145–57.

33. The so-called Antinomian Controversy (of 1636–1638)— subtly evoked by Hawthorne's sketch of "Mrs. Hutchinson" (1830)— settled the point that, despite the public objections of Ann Hutchinson and the fine distinctions of John Cotton, "sanctification" (the observable ability to obey divine law) would clearly follow as a proper effect of "justification" (the private revelation of a person's acceptance by God); see Miller, *Seventeenth Century*, pp. 389–92; Edmund S. Morgan, *Puritan Dilemma* (Boston: Little Brown, 1958), pp. 134–54; and William K. B. Stoever, *A Faire and Easie Way to Heaven* (Middletown, CT: Wesleyan University Press, 1978), esp. pp. 21–33. For application of these concerns to YGB, see James W. Matthews, "Antinomianism in YGB," *Studies in Short Fiction* 3 (1965), 73–5; Claudia G. Johnson, "YGB and Puritan Justification," *Studies in Short Fiction* 11 (1974), 200–3; and Jane Donahue Eberwein, "'My Faith is Gone': YGB and Puritan Conversion," *Christianity and Literature* 32 (1982), 23–32.

34. For the uniqueness of the "congregational" polity, see Miller, *Seventeenth Century*, pp. 432–62; and Edmund S. Morgan, *Visible Saints* (Ithaca: Cornell University Press, 1963), pp. 1–112. The remnants of this system lasted well into Hawthorne's own century, but the basis of his scholarly knowledge of the problem may well have been Book 5 ("Acts and Monuments of the Faith and Order in the Churches of New England") of Cotton Mather's *Magnalia Christi Americana* (London, 1702).

35. Though Miller implies that the Puritans' "subjective insight" and "obsession with individuality" (*Seventeenth Century*, p. 22) are balanced by their sense of the particular church as "the center of a communal system" where "the fraternity was made one by their mutual and irrevocable pledge" (p. 443), we still lack a convincing account of the overwhelming commitment to community we sense in the pages of Bradford's *Plymouth Plantation* and Winthrop's "Model of Christian Charity." For the best available study of the social dynamics of the profession of "saving faith"— made for the judgment and edification of the entire congregation—see Patricia Caldwell, *The Puritan Conversion Narrative* (Cambridge: Cambridge University Press, 1983), esp. pp. 45–116.

36. See "Shadows of Doubt: Specter Evidence in Hawthorne's YGB," *American Literature* 34 (1962), 344–52. Levin provides an extremely useful collection of texts and documents related to the "spectral" question of 1692 in *What Happened in Salem* (New York: Harcourt, Brace & World, 1960). For a full-scale account of YGB as a crisis in the Puritan theory of evidence, see Colacurcio, *Province*, pp. 283–313 (bibliography, pp. 610–17). And for an attempt to generalize the notion of spectrality to cover the question of history, see Budick, *Historical Consciousness*, pp. 79–97.

37. This "undecidability" lends some credence to a "postmodern" reading; see, for example, Christopher D. Morris, "Deconstructing YGB," *American Transcendental Quarterly* 2 (1988), 22–33. And yet, as Goodman Brown is forced to make *some* decision, the story appears to concern faith more properly than signifiers. Clearly (in any case) it is shortsighted to claim that the issue of specter evidence causes us to blame the Devil and excuse Goodman Brown; see Paul J. Hurley, "YGB's 'Heart of Darkness,'" *New England Quarterly* 37 (1966), 410

38. See Stanley Cavell, *In Quest of the Ordinary* (Chicago: University of Chicago Press, 1988), p. 55.

39. For Spenser's influence on Hawthorne's theme of specter evidence, see John Schroeder, "Alice Doane's Story: An Essay on Hawthorne and Spenser," *Nathaniel Hawthorne Journal* 4 (1974), 129–34; and Colacurcio, *Province*, pp. 84–5, 295–7.

40. For the inceptive version of the nineteenth-century view of the Salem witchcraft as a combination of outmoded superstition and the deleterious influence of Cotton Mather, see Charles W. Upham, *Lectures on Witchcraft* (Boston, 1831).

# Chronology

| | |
|---|---|
| 1804 | Born in Salem, Massachusetts. |
| 1808 | Hawthorne's father dies of yellow fever, and Hawthorne's mother mourns him in seclusion. |
| 1813 | Restricted in activities by a foot injury, and thus encouraged in his reading. |
| 1818 | Moves with mother and sisters to land inherited from the Mannings at Raymond, Maine. |
| 1821–1825 | Attends Bowdoin College with Franklin Pierce and Henry Wadsworth Longfellow. |
| 1825 | Returns to the "chamber under the eaves" in his mother's house in Salem and spends a dozen years of relative seclusion, reading and writing, rather than entering a trade or profession. |
| 1828 | *Fanshawe* (published anonymously at his own expense). |
| 1830 | Published in the *Salem Gazette* his first story, "The Hollow of the Three Hills." |
| 1836 | Edits *American Magazine of Useful and Entertaining Knowledge*. |
| 1837 | Publishes *Twice-Told Tales*. |
| 1837 | Compiles *Peter Parley's Universal History*. |
| 1839–40 | Becomes engaged to Sophia Peabody, daughter of Dr. Nathaniel and Amelia Peabody; works for Boston Custom House. |

| | |
|---|---|
| 1841 | Publishes *Grandfather's Chair; Famous Old People; Liberty Tree*. |
| 1841 | Joins Brook Farm Community at West Roxbury, Massachusetts; invests $1,500 in the venture, but withdraws before the end of the year. |
| 1842 | Marries Sophia Peabody. |
| 1842–45 | Lives at the Old Manse, Concord, where he has as neighbors and associates Emerson, Thoreau, Margaret Fuller, and Amos Bronson Alcott; daughter Una born. |
| 1842 | Publishes *Twice-Told Tales* (enlarged); *Biographical Stories for Children*. |
| 1846 | Publishes *Mosses from an Old Manse*; becomes surveyor for the Port of Salem, where he earns $1,200 a year; son Julian born. |
| 1849 | Leaves Port of Salem; death of his mother occurs while he is writing *The Scarlet Letter*. |
| 1850 | Publishes *The Scarlet Letter*, bringing fame and recognition. |
| 1851 | Moves to Lenox in Western Massachusetts; publishes *The House of the Seven Gables, The Snow-Image and Other Twice-Told Tales*, and *True Stories from History and Biography*; May 20, daughter Rose born. |
| 1852 | Moves to West Newton, Massachusetts; publishes *The Blithedale Romance, A Wonder Book* and a campaign biography of Franklin Pierce; moves to the Wayside, Concord. |
| 1853 | Publishes *Tanglewood Tales* for children. |
| 1853–1857 | Appointed by President Pierce to serve as United States Consul at Liverpool, England. |
| 1858 | Resigns consul; lives in Rome and Florence; frequents art museums and writes extended notebook entries which he later reworks for inclusion in *The Marble Faun*. |
| 1860 | Returns to Concord; publishes *The Marble Faun*; strives to finish another romance and at his death leaves four fragments: *Dr. Grimshawe's Secret, Septimius Felton, The Ancestral Footstep*, and *The Doliver Romance*. |

1862          March-April, visits Horatio Bridge in Washington, D.C.; calls on President Lincoln; writes "Chiefly About War Matters."

1863          Publishes *Our Old Home*.

1864          April 10, shaken by the death of his friend W. D. Ticknor; May 11, accompanies Pierce to New Hampshire; May 19, dies at Plymouth, New Hampshire. May 23, is buried at Sleepy Hollow Cemetery, Concord.

# Works by Nathaniel Hawthorne

*The Scarlet Letter*, 1850.

*The House of the Seven Gables*, 1851.

*The Blithedale Romance*, 1852.

*The Marble Faun*, 1860.

*Twice-Told Tales*, 1837, 1851.

*Mosses from an Old Manse*, 1846, 1854.

*The Snow-Image, and Other Twice-Told Tales*, 1852.

*The Life of Franklin Pierce*, 1852.

"Chiefly About War Matters," 1862.

*Our Old Home: A Series of English Sketches*, 1863.

*The Whole History of Grandfather's Chair*, 1840.

*A Wonder-Book for Girls and Boys*, 1852.

*Tanglewood Tales*, 1853.

# Works about Nathaniel Hawthorne

Abel, Darrel. *The Moral Picturesque: Studies in Hawthorne's Fiction*. West Lafayette, Indiana: Purdue University Press, 1988.

Brodhead, Richard H. *Hawthorne, Melville, and the Novel*. Chicago and London: University of Chicago Press, 1976.

Bell, Millicent. *Hawthorne's View of the Artist*. Albany: State University of New York, c1962.

———. *New Essays on Hawthorne's Major Tales*. Cambridge and New York: Cambridge University Press, 1993.

Crews, Frederick C. *The Sins of the Fathers: Hawthorne's Psychological Themes*. New York: Oxford University Press, 1966.

Curl, Vega. *Pasteboard Masks: Fact as a Spiritual Symbol in the Novels of Hawthorne and Melville*. Cambridge: Harvard University Press, 1931.

Davidson, Edward Hutchins. *Hawthorne's Last Phase*. New Haven: Yale University Press, 1949.

Donohue, Agnes McNeill. *Hawthorne: Calvin's Ironic Stepchild*. Kent, OH: The Kent State University Press, 1985.

Doubleday, Neal Frank. *Hawthorne's Early Tales: A Critical Study*. Durham: Duke University Press, 1972.

Dunne, Michael. *Hawthorne's Narrative Strategies*. Jackson: University Press of Mississippi, 1995.

Elder, Marjorie J. *Nathaniel Hawthorne, Transcendental Symbolist*. Athens: University Press, 1969.

Fairbanks, Henry George. *The Lasting Loneliness of Nathaniel Hawthorne: A Study of the Sources of Alienation in Modern Man*. Albany: Magi Books, 1965.

Fogle, Richard Harter. *Hawthorne's Fiction: The Light and the Dark*. Norman: University of Oklahoma Press, 1964.

Fossum, Robert H. *Hawthorne's Inviolable Circle: The Problem of Time*. Deland: Everett/Edwards, 1972.

Goode, Diane. *Rumpty Dudget's Tower, Based on the Fairy Tale by Julian Hawthorne*. New York: Knopf, 1987.

Hall, Lawrence Sargent. *Hawthorne: Critic of Society*. New Haven: Yale University Press and London: Oxford University Press, 1944.

Idol, Jr., John L. and Buford Jone, eds. *Nathaniel Hawthorne: The Contemporary Reviews*. Cambridge: Cambridge University Press, 1994.

James, Henry. *Hawthorne*. New York: Harper and Brothers, 1880.

Kent, Deborah. *Salem, Massachusetts*. Parsippany, NJ: Dillon Press, 1996.

Laffrado, Laura. *Hawthorne's Literature for Children*, Athens, GA. and London: The University of Georgia Press, 1992.

Levin, Harry. *The Power of Blackness: Hawthorne, Poe, Melville*. New York: Knopf, 1958.

Lundblad, Jane. *Nathaniel Hawthorne and European Literary Tradition*. Cambridge, MA: Harvard University Press, 1947.

Mancall, James N. *"Thoughts Painfully Intense": Hawthorne and the Invalid Author*. New York & London: Routledge, 2002.

Manley, Seon. *Nathaniel Hawthorne: Captain of the Imagination*. New York: Vanguard Press 1968.

Miller, Edwin Haviland. *Salem Is My Dwelling Place: A Life of Nathaniel Hawthorne*. Iowa City: University of Iowa Press, 1991.

Miller, J. Hillis. *Hawthorne and History: Defacing It*. Cambridge, MA and Oxford: Basil Blackwell, 1991.

Moore, Thomas R. *A Thick and Darksome Veil: The Rhetoric of Hawthorne's Sketches, Prefaces, and Essays*. Boston: Northeastern University Press, 1994.

Price-Groff, Claire. *Extrodinary Women Journalists (Margaret Fuller)*. New York: Children's Press, 1997.

Schoonmaker, Frances, Editor. *Henry W. Longfellow*. New York: Sterling Publishers, 1998.

Schubert, Leland. *Hawthorne the Artist: Fine-art Devices in Fiction*. New York: Russell & Russell, 1963 [c1944].

Sheckman, Richard. *Presidential Ambition (Franklin Pierce)*. New York: HarperCollins, 1999.

Smith, Harmon L. *My Friend, My Friend: The Story of Thoreau's Relationship with Emerson*. Amherst: University of Massachusetts Press, 1999.

Stein, William Bysshe. *Hawthorne's Faust, A Study of the Devil Archetype*. Gainesville: University of Florida Press, 1953.

Stoehr, Taylor. *Hawthorne's Mad Scientists: Pseudoscience and Social Science in Nineteenth-Century Life and Letters*, Hamden, CT: Archon Books. 1978.

Stowe, William W. *Going Abroad, European Travel in Nineteenth-Century American Culture*. Princeton: Princeton University Press, 1994.

Swisher, Clarice, ed., *Readings on Nathaniel Hawthorne*. San Diego: Greenhaven Press, 1996.

Taylor, Bob Pepperman. *America's Bachelor Uncle: Thoreau and the American Polity*. Lawrence: University Press of Kansas, 1996.

Taylor, J. Golden. *Hawthorne's Ambivalence toward Puritanism*. Norwood, PA.: Norwood Editions, 1978 [c1965].

Tharpe, Jac. *Nathaniel Hawthorne: Identity and Knowledge*. Carbondale: Southern Illinois University Press, 1967.

Turner, Arlin. *Nathaniel Hawthorne: an Introduction and Interpretation*. New York: Barnes & Noble, 1961.

Van Doren, Mark. *Nathaniel Hawthorne*. New York: William Sloane Associates, Inc., 1949.

Wagenknecht, Edward. *Nathaniel Hawthorne: The Man, His Tales, and Romances*. New York : Continuum, 1988.

# Contributors

HAROLD BLOOM is Sterling Professor of the Humanities at Yale University and Henry W. and Albert A. Berg Professor of English at the New York University Graduate School. He is the author of over 20 books, including *Shelley's Mythmaking* (1959), *The Visionary Company* (1961), *Blake's Apocalypse* (1963), *Yeats* (1970), *A Map of Misreading* (1975), *Kabbalah and Criticism* (1975), *Agon: Toward a Theory of Revisionism* (1982), *The American Religion* (1992), *The Western Canon* (1994), and *Omens of Millennium: The Gnosis of Angels, Dreams, and Resurrection* (1996). *The Anxiety of Influence* (1973) sets forth Professor Bloom's provocative theory of the literary relationships between the great writers and their predecessors. His most recent books include *Shakespeare: The Invention of the Human* (1998), a 1998 National Book Award finalist, *How to Read and Why* (2000), and *Genius: A Mosaic of One Hundred Exemplary Creative Minds* (2002). In 1999, Professor Bloom received the prestigious American Academy of Arts and Letters Gold Medal for Criticism, and in 2002 he received the Catalonia International Prize.

NORMA JEAN LUTZ is a freelance writer who lives in Tulsa, Oklahoma. Writing professionally since 1977, she is the author of more than 250 short stories and articles as well as 50-plus books—fiction and nonfiction.

NEIL HEIMS is a freelance writer, editor, and researcher. He has a Ph.D. in English from the City University of New York.

HENRY JAMES is considered to be one of the greatest American novelists of the 20th century, as well as a world renown playright and critic. His works include *The Portrait of a Lady*, *Washington Square*, *The Wings of the Dove*, and *The Golden Bowl*.

MICHAEL J. COLACURCIO is Professor of English at the University of California, Los Angeles. His books include *The Province of Piety: Moral History in Hawthorne's Early Tales*, and *New Essays on "The Scarlet Letter"*.

# INDEX